The Kingdom Weigh

Health for your
Spirit, Soul & Body

Rev. Cathy Dickson
Health Minister

The Kingdom Weigh
Copyright © 2014 by Rev. Cathy Dickson

Dedication

To those I love, my Lord and Saviour Jesus Christ and to all of those who have toiled relentlessly to bring love, hope, and strength to people of all nations.

I honor my parents and mentors who have gone before me and present this book as a foundation for the generations to come after me.

May you truly be blessed, strengthened and inspired as you read and follow the principles of The Kingdom Weigh. Truly you will be transformed from the inside out and discover your destiny within these pages.

Your humble servant,

Rev. Cathy Dickson

Rev. Cathy Dickson
www.mamaCD.org

Table of Contents

INTRODUCTION

 Greetings to my brothers, sisters and friends from around the world; my name is (Reverend) Cathy Dickson. First and foremost I'm a child of the Kingdom of God; my life experience, education, Masters in Biblical Studies, BA with health sciences and social sciences, and almost ½ century of ministry experience pales to the experiences that the Lord has brought me through that have led me to today. My credentials are not my ordination as a Teacher with Apostolic Mantle; registration to Solemnize Marriages or my registration with the College of Social Workers and Social Service Workers; my credentials are a Child of the Kingdom of Heaven—the Church of which most of you are likely a part of me and I of you.

I've been very blessed to have been raised by two God fearing parents, both actively involved in ministry and have continued throughout my life to walk in immeasurably blessing, and entertainment at times, with eight children, 9+ grandchildren and many, many spiritual children, too great a number to count. Currently I teach in a college a program for those who wish to work in Social Services as well as teach at various locations around the world as the Lord directs; such as here today.

I have a message that is timely, relevant and life changing for all who have an ear to hear what the Spirit of the Lord will speak to them today. That message transforms the mind, delivers the soul and heals the body. God's called us to peace within, but the cares of this world have stolen that peace from so many of us, the stresses cause us great anguish and threaten our very core essence of faith, but through it all know that God has not left you; He is re-

5

aligning you as a Kingdom citizen for His great end time purposes for your life. Rejoice and be exceedingly glad for the Lord thy God is with you. I promise you, His plans for you are for good and not evil. You may not see it just yet, but as you draw close to Him and continue in His ways, He will reveal greatness to you and through you. Always remember that it took Jesus 30 years to be prepared for His 3 years of ministry and He had the greatest ministry ever demonstrated on this earth, thus far. The greater ministry will come as God unites His Church to do the work that its destined to do. We are the Church!

This Workshop and Booklet were birthed from the heart of God. For years as I've taught or shared a story from my own life with others, inevitably people would say, "you should write a book". I pondered the idea but thought that my writing wasn't good enough, yet from time to time, I'd jot down thoughts and I've kept a journal of revelation from the Lord so there is a lot of information and revelation floating around in my 3lb brain.

Recently, I received a couple of personal prophetic words from seasoned prophets. That just means that God spoke through another person, and my spirit bore witness to what they were saying. They spoke of me writing and teaching. I felt convicted, for I've had that word many, many times through prophets from around the world yet I've put very little effort into doing it. The Lord reminded me that 20 or more years ago I received a prophetic word on teaching, and I thought they were "off their rocker", who me? How could I teach? I'm way too shy; I can barely lift my head or speak to strangers. To make a long story short, today I'm a college instructor for a terrific group of young adults. At that reminder I decided to put my fingers to the keyboard and start writing.

First of all, I went to the Lord and asked Him what to write about. Should I write an autobiography? Trust me! That would address pretty much most of the issues of life that you've dealt with. I just don't like to talk about me, unless I know it will benefit the person who is listening. I felt that the Lord wanted me to address some of the health issues that plague the church today. I too have struggled with and overcome many health issues, some of which were rooted in obesity. In fact I lost over 100lbs and other than a few emotional battles along the way where I lost my focus for a time, I've kept it off for the past 7 years. This was the answer; God gave me an answer that changed my life, as I pray this book will change yours also.

Next, I started to write, but it was so jumbled. I became frustrated it was as if 500 potential books were hitting me from all angles at the same time. At that point I stopped, put it away and just prayed for direction. I had a dream, which I do vividly almost nightly. This night I was reading the words of the book. When I woke up, I got distracted and didn't write the dream down immediately like I normally do. After a few minutes, I said, "Oh God, I can't remember what was written on the pages, I need you to show me, Please!" The Lord didn't just give me another picture of the words; although a vision would have been interesting and I thought it might have been very helpful. Instead he just spoke to me, as He does regularly. He said, "just start writing and I will complete the good work that you began".

And so it is that this book was born. I pray that as you read it that the eyes and ears of your understanding would be opened, your heart receptive through humility to recognize your weakness and through the pages of this book find Him who is your strength to overcome the battles that rage within you, and sometimes around you.

May God truly bless you as you read and overcome!

Reverend Cathy Dickson, Health Minister

www.MamaCD.org

The Kingdom Weigh
Weekly Agenda Overview

A 12 week Spiritual Weight Loss & Life Energizing Program based on Biblical Principles focusing on the Bread of Life not rules and regulations of what, where, when, how or why to eat certain foods.

"Seek first the Kingdom of God and his righteousness, and all these things will be added to you" (Mt 6:33)

<u>**Weekly Agenda** *2-4-U*</u> *(2 hours for yourself; 2 hours for freedom from bondages)*

30 minutes: Weigh-in (optional); Journal & Home Work Sharing

60 minutes: Spiritual Weight Loss Strategies Lesson & Discussion

30 minutes: Homework Assignment; Q & A

<u>**Weekly Topics and Home Work**</u>

1. **Confronting Excuses**: "but they all alike began to make excuses…" Luke 14:18-20; Moses said, "Oh, my Lord, I am not eloquent in speech …" "therefore you have no excuse, o man, everyone who judges.. for in passing judgement on another you condemn yourself, because you, the judge, practice the very same things" Rom 2:1; Ex 4: 10-14; "my people perish for lack of vision" Prov 29:18; "In you, Lord my God, I put my trust" Ps 25:1

Homework My Excuses vs What God Says Chart

2. **Goal Setting:** "-"Where there is no prophetic vision the people cast off restraint, but blessed is the one who heeds wisdom's instruction" (Prov 29:18).

   Homework Creating a Vision Board

3. **Portion Distortion**: "Honest weights and balances belong to the Lord; he sets the standards for fairness". (Prov 16:11). "A false balance is an abomination to the Lord: but a just weight is his delight

   Homework Journal for 7days Record all eating occasions honestly. Did you stay within God Given Boundaries?

4. **Gardening: Pulling out the Roots of Overindulgence**: breaking off generational curses, habits, addictions, fears "If we confess our sins He is faithful and just to forgive us our sins..."1 John 1:9; "There is therefore now no condemnation to them which are in Christ Jesus, who walk not after the flesh, but after the Spirit. For the law of the Spirit of life in Christ Jesus hath made me free from the law of sin and death." Romans 8:1-2; "...Forgive, and you will be forgiven" Luke 6:37

   Homework Breaking Free of Generational Curses, Habits, Addictions and Fears checklist guide for personal prayer (confession, denouncing sins, re-alignment)

5. **The Best Food**: physical nutritional and diet plans discussed; pros-cons; Canada's Food Guide;

Bible/Rainbow/Genesis Diet; Vegan, Vegetarian, Low Carb, Paleo comparisons
Spiritual Diet- Jesus said, "my food is to do the will of Him who sent me, and to finish His work" John 4:34

Homework Revelation Scripture or Bible story that the Holy Spirit speaks to you regarding food, eating, Spirit led life etc. (to be shared next week with group)

6. **Pharoah's Control vs. Freedom**: 10 plagues of Egypt (natural mind)—the 10 thought patterns that keep us in bondage ending with the death of the first born, our Adamic nature (sin/flesh nature) Plagues of Blood, frogs, gnats, flies, against livestock, boils, hail, locusts, darkness, firstborn. Exodus 7
Homework Identifying each plague in your mind (self-talk) that has kept you in bondage until now

7. **Our Vision, Purpose & Destiny**: thought, emotions, actions, habits, prophetic words, hobbies, education. Identifying your purpose & destiny and discovering the path to fulfillment. "Where there is no prophetic vision, the people cast off restraint" Prov 29:18

Homework Emotional Log;

8. **Law & Order**: diet rules (law) or Spirit led (order)=Freedom in Christ; Taking back self-control with Blossoming Fruit "Christ Jesus has set you free from the law of sin and death" Rom 8:2

Homework Write your Spiritual Mission Statement

11

9. **LOVE-covers a multitude of sins; Ego vs Altruism**: learning to love yourself and treat yourself with God's love, not anger, punishment but joy in the Holy Spirit; " speaking the truth in love, growing in every way more and more like Christ" Eph 4:15

   Homework Daily look in your own eyes in the mirror and let the Spirit of the Lord speak through you to you, "I love you…" (add affirmations of who you are in Christ) Journal your reactions

10. **Bumps, Road blocks, Stumbling and Pride:** Expect opposition, be ready in season and out of season; "stay alert! Watch out for your great enemy, the devil. He prowls around like a roaring lion, looking for someone to devour" 1 Peter 5:8; "No temptation has overtaken you but such as is common to man; and God is faithful, who will not allow you to be tempted beyond what you are able, but with the temptation will provide the way of escape also, so that you will be able to endure it." 1 Cor 10:13

    Homework record the ways of escape that God made this week

11. **Co-creators of our Destiny**: spirit-soul-body connection; God gives us the desires of our heart (those desires that are placed there by God) Mind/Will/Emotional entrainment to the desires of your heart Ps 37:4; "what I fear most overtakes me. What I dread happens to me" Job 3:25

12. Overcomers!: Testimony of what the Lord has done in your life through this program. How have you grown in your spirit, mind, will, emotions? How much weight have you let go of over these past 12 weeks? Graph or record your weight loss below.

Wt	# 1	#2	#3	#4	#5	#6	#7	#8	#9	# 10	# 11	# 12

THE KINGDOM WEIGH GROUP GUIDELINES

- There is *no condemnation*, we are all at different places on our walk with God, this is not about size, starving, or even eating by a prescribed set of rules. This is about heart restoration and freedom in Christ

- *No judgments.* for the same measure that you judge you will be judged. When we look at another person and recognize a shortcoming, we only see a reflection of the shortcomings in ourselves. Often it's the very thing that we recognize in another that is our own stumbling block.

- *No rules, no regulations, no bondage.* Each person will discover their own guidelines for their nutritional needs or ideal weight by God's wisdom within. Sharing nutritional tips that apply to yourself, may not be what the other person needs. Let's remain sensitive to each member's needs so that they can conform to Christ's image, not our image.

- *We are One Body.* We're in this together, we're intimately connected in the Spirit, therefore what affects you, affects me. Pray one for another that we would all be healed.

- *Humility, forgiveness are keys to freedom.* As you feel safe you, or someone in the group may share some very personal information, out of respect for our body (the body of Christ) Please keep that information solely between you and the Father in prayer as He leads you to pray.

- ***Celebration!*** Although weigh-ins are optional. Let's celebrate successes, not only in weight loss, but in any accomplishment that leads one of us closer to our goals.

- ***Disclaimer:*** Any person who is currently under medical supervision for a metabolic disorder or any disorder requiring medication or special diets should consult with and update their physician as they progress. Medication dosages may need to be reduced under your physician's direction.

CONFRONTING EXCUSES

What's the first thing that comes to your mind when you ask someone to do something? Perhaps you ask your child or close loved one and they continue to make excuses. Does it irritate you? anger you? make you want to disassociate with the excuse maker, perhaps confuse you? How do you think God responds to excuses from His children? Does it make you want to go above and beyond to compensate for that person's lack of motivation to change? (If that's the case we need to talk about co-dependency) Think about it, what is effect of excuses in your life? For most it gets them out of doing what they don't want to do. It's a simple battle between what our Flesh/Self/Sin nature wants and what God wants. That's it in a nutshell!

Trust me, I'm an experienced excuse maker, over half a century of proven excuse making in many different areas. The first remembrance of excuses that I'm going to talk about is my childhood experience, because I was the queen of excuses. When my mother would ask me to do something that was even remotely challenging I would respond with a quick, whiny excuse, "I can't". Quickly my mother would answer and say, "Can't doesn't exist". She never let me get away with saying "I can't". "I can" or "I'll try my best" is a much better answer. As I mentioned, I'm a college instructor, I've heard almost every excuse possible. "The dog ate my paper"; "I had no clothes washed, so I couldn't come to school"; "my grandmother died (again, she forgot that she used that excuse twice already)" or "I didn't know we had to do that" Of course it's been on the board and I've explained it umpteen times plus given the student a clearly written description of the assignment. You see as a teacher, I pretty much know when the excuse is really a cover up for a deeper issue.

Often an excuse is easier than telling the truth of our own personal short coming. God knows implicitly when we offer him excuses whether spoken out loud or in our hearts; He know if they're merely expressions of laziness, selfishness or fear. As we proceed through this lesson open your heart up to what the Lord will speak to you regarding your excuses. As those excuses are brought to the light (truth) they will no longer hold their power over you.

One of my favourite examples in the Word of God is the Wedding Banquet parable told by Jesus " *When one of those who sat at table with him heard this, he said to him, "Blessed is he who shall eat bread in the kingdom of God!" But he said to him, "A man once gave a great banquet, and invited many; and at the time for the banquet he sent his servant to say to those who had been invited, `Come; for all is now ready.' But they all alike began to make excuses. The first said to him, `I have bought a field, and I must go out and see it; I pray you, have me excused.' And another said, `I have bought five yoke of oxen, and I go to examine them; I pray you, have me excused.' And another said, `I have married a wife, and therefore I cannot come.' So the servant came and reported this to his master. Then the householder in anger said to his servant, `Go out quickly to the streets and lanes of the city, and bring in the poor and maimed and blind and lame.' And the servant said, `Sir,* *what you commanded has been done, and still there is room.' And the master said to the servant, 'Go out to the highways and hedges, and compel people to come in, that my house may be filled. For I tell you, none of those men who were invited shall taste my banquet.'" (Luke 14:15-24) (Mt 22:1-14)*

A royal wedding banquet given by the King of kings; the most important banquet of all, yet people make excuses as to why they can't be there. Where is the fear of God, the beginning of wisdom? How about ourselves, have we too made excuses to the King?

The last book in the Bible ends with an invitation to the wedding feast of the Lamb and his Bride, the church: *The Spirit and the Bride say, Come! (Rev. 22:17)*. In this parable, Jesus' invited guests made excuses as to why they couldn't come. It must have been like a slap in the King's face for the invited guests to refuse the invitation. They couldn't come because they put their own interests above those of the King.

Jesus asks the reasons why people made excuses to the greatest banquet invitation. The first person with an excuse says that their business takes precedence over God's desire. The second excuse allows personal goods or possessions to come before God. The third excuse puts home and family ahead of God. God never meant for our home and relationships to be used selfishly. We serve God best when we invite him into our work and homes and when we share our possessions with others.

Since the guests had too many excuses the attention is turned to those who were rejected; the ."poor, maimed, blind, and lame", the outcasts of society -- those who can make no claim on the King. Of course this refers to the gentiles. This is certainly an invitation of grace --

undeserved, unmerited favor and kindness! But this invitation also contains a warning for those who refuse it or who approach the wedding feast unworthily. Grace is a free gift, but it is also an awesome responsibility. Some consider a "cheap grace", but the truth is that it is a very "costly grace". Cheap grace is the grace we bestow on ourselves, such as in the preaching of forgiveness without requiring repentance or grace without discipleship, grace without the cross, or even grace without following Jesus Christ. I've seen some who feel it's okay to do what they want because we're covered by God's grace. You know what I mean, smoke up Saturday night and show up Sunday morning. Abuse your spouse and then preach or teach Sunday school. These things ought not to be and to change it begins with me.

Cheap grace is a gross misinterpretation of the Holy Scriptures. Grace never came cheap, it cost Jesus everything and it costs us everything. That's why we must count the cost of following the Lord. Salvation costs you nothing, but developing into Christ-like-ness will cost you everything. Salvation occurs at the instant of accepting Jesus as your Saviour, but becoming mature in Christ takes a lifetime. Growing up into all things takes time and obedience. It's not burdensome, nor striving, but a necessary step to come into the fullness of what God wants for us as an individual and as the Bride of Christ. If you claim to be a Kingdom Citizen, then do not quit, nor waste your years. The only thing that you truly have to spend is not money, but it's time. Currency is simply an exchange for time. Make sure that your time on earth counts for the Kingdom of God. God's grace costs us a surrendering of our will for His, giving our lives to Him for His purpose; dying to our ego, our self/sin/flesh nature and staying alive unto Him. He promises to give you back more than you ever give up. He gives freedom from the slavery that your ego tries to hold on to. Just surrender all!

Lord, no good gift do you withhold from those who walk uprightly. Help me to seek your kingdom first and to lay aside anything that might hinder me from doing your will."

Here's the excuse that many Christians throw out without reading the entire passage they quote Paul who used the excuse that it's sin within him that makes him do the things that he doesn't want to do, so the things that he wants to do he doesn't. In Romans 7 & 8 he describes his struggle with sin and says he is a slave to sin. This is where Christians stop reading to justify their sinful habits, yet in Romans 8 he goes on to say that *"we are no longer controlled by our sinful nature but rather by the Spirit of God that lives in us"*. We have no excuses, for we can do all things through Christ who strengthens us.

Other excuses in the Bible are found in:

But I can't *"And they all with one [consent] began to make excuse. The first said unto him, I have bought a piece of ground, and I must needs go and see it: I pray thee have me excused"* *(Luke 14:18-20)*

I lost my... *"And he said unto another, Follow me. But he said, Lord, suffer me first to go and bury my father. (Luke 9:59-62)*

I'm not smart enough *"And Moses said unto the LORD, O my Lord, I [am] not eloquent, neither heretofore, nor since thou hast spoken unto thy servant: but I [am] slow of speech, and of a slow tongue. (Ex 4:10-14)*

Projecting Blame *"And the LORD God said unto the woman, What [is] this [that] thou hast done? And the*

21

woman said, The serpent beguiled me, and I did eat. (Gen 3:13)

I'm a college professor, I've heard every excuse from dogs eating paper, to the same person dying 2 or 3 times in the same year. Our Adamic nature projects blame: We make excuses for our bad behaviour. It's not your spouse, your circumstances, your children, your employer or friend that made you do anything. It's sin nature—your Adamic nature within you. As a 16 year old I was pulled over for speeding. When asked by the officer why I was going 40 mph in a 30mph zone I quickly, blamed my boyfriend for making me mad, I took no responsibility for my foot on the gas pedal. Think for a moment of some excuses that you've used, perhaps excuses that you've given God for why you can't be a healthy weigh—your genes, medication, stress. Genes are like a blueprint, it's the architect that expresses the blueprint. In other words genes do not determine your weight, your choices in your environment do. Medications can cause weight gain, but perhaps the medication can be changed, reduced, or you can be honest with what you are eating while on the medication to reduce its negative side effects, rather than indulging in the cakes, cookies, chips, ice-cream or huge portion sizes only to use medication as your excuse for gaining weight.

Inexcusable judgement *"Therefore thou art inexcusable, O man, whosoever thou art that judgest: for wherein thou judgest another, thou condemnest thyself; for thou that judgest doest the same things." (Rom 2:1-29)*

God's Patience in our growth *"The Lord is not slack concerning his promise, as some men count slackness; but is longsuffering to us-ward, not willing that any should perish, but that all should come to repentance" (2 Peter*

3:9)

Who is your father? God or Satan? *"Not every one that saith unto me, Lord, Lord, shall enter into the kingdom of heaven; but he that doeth the will of my Father which is in heaven"* *(Mt7:21)*

New Creature *"Therefore if any man [be] in Christ, [he is] a new creature: old things are passed away; behold, all things are become new" (2 Cor 5:17)*

Be Honest with yourself *"A false witness shall not be unpunished, and [he that] speaketh lies shall not escape." (Prov19:5)*

God corrects you because He loves you *"All scripture [is] given by inspiration of God, and [is] profitable for doctrine, for reproof, for correction, for instruction in righteousness"* *(2Tim3:16)*

Be separated unto God *"Paul, a servant of Jesus Christ, called [to be] an apostle, separated unto the gospel of God, (Rom 1:1-32)*

Excuses are not new they are as old as the garden of Eden yet just as powerfully sinful, proud and disobedient as they were at first. They've hindered God's best in people's lives throughout the Word of God, and even now continue to hinder God's best for His people until this day. May God grant us eyes to see, ears to hear and a heart to receive what the spirit of the Lord is speaking to us today. This day, let's become followers of Christ as Paul was, separated unto the good news which includes our freedom from the bondages of sin and death. Greed is sin; taking in more food than what our body's need is sin and not listening to the voice of the Lord deliberately for the purpose of self-gratifying indulgence is sin. This week, through obedience to the voice of the Lord we'll examine our eating and begin to re-align our appetites with the appetite that He has designed for each one of us. Let's purpose before the Lord to heed the voice of God and eat with an honest balance through the natural hunger/fullness mechanism God has given us.

Learning to eat *(or whatever your struggle is)* as God ordained for you is like riding a bicycle, some people learn to ride easily, the first time they hop on, they've got it and never or rarely fall off. Some individuals struggle more, their balance is not good, they fall many times but with persistence, love and patience with themselves and their cheering section they will succeed to ride that bicycle. Even accomplished riders, the best riders in the world fall from time to time. There is no judgement in falling, but there is a fearful judgement before the Lord for wilfully choosing not to get up again on that "spiritual" bike and start peddling. He's holding you up in every endeavour that you do to honor Him. Do not fear, you will not fail, you are not a failure. The only failure is giving up!

Over these next few weeks we're going to look at how our selfish eating habits, clouded in excuses, hinder us from God's best in our lives, and potentially keep us from fulfilling our destiny as He designed for us.

The function of an excuse is basically to shift blame away from ourselves to another person, quality or circumstance that we convince ourselves cannot be changed. If it's not our fault, but rather our genes, our meds, our socio-economic status, then we can't be blamed. That protects our self-image and helps us feel good about ourselves despite our behaviours that lead to obesity or whatever type of bondage besets you. Although it guards our self-image it also promotes a sense of helplessness that we accept as our identity. It tarnishes our testimony as our witness for God is weakened. How can a God that is so great not help you put the fork *(cigarette, bottle, anger, pornography)* down?

Excuse making is closely tied to low self-esteem, a lack of self-respect; incompetence and blamelessness, how can anyone blame us for the problem, it's not our fault...we have excuses. Surely giving excuses to God shows a lack of respect for Him too. The solution to excuse making is to take responsibility for the problem, to stop immediately putting the blame on anyone or anything other than on ourselves. It's not our parents fault, it's not the food's fault, medication's fault, stress or circumstances, lack of time, wrong foods available, or any other excuse that you might want to use. If you are struggling with your weight it is 100% your fault. Stop blaming, start aiming for your true self, your true nature, you're God nature within you. The problem will leave and you will arise to fulfill your destiny.

"Success isn't arriving at something from a journey out there, it's when you find yourself and find your purpose in life from your exploration within yourself. Until you find yourself you will always be someone else. Become yourself." (Dr. Myles Munroe)

Follow the three R's:

1. **R**espect for God, self, others

2. **R**epenting of sin

3. **R**esponsibility for all your actions.

Imagine for a moment the beautiful princess waiting to be rescued by the handsome prince, but when the prince arrives and calls her out, she says, I'd love to come but I'm not ready yet, I've got to put some makeup on first, or whatever lame excuse she may have. Just like the 5 wise and 5 foolish virgins. 5 were ready for the bridegroom, they had their oil for their lamps, with no excuse necessary they were ready and arose to go with the bridegroom. The foolish however had excuses why they couldn't come, their excuse was that they weren't ready because their lamps were going out, they didn't have extra oil, however the truth was that they didn't believe that he would arrive at that hour so they procrastinated. This day is a day that God no longer wants excuses from His people, procrastination is an excuse. The foolish virgin procrastinated. The bride in Solomon chapter 5 procrastinated. Procrastinating is not taking responsibility for our time and actions and can have very costly consequences. He wants us to be prepared in season and out of season. To be equipped for service and to become all that He wants through surrendering to His will and answering when He calls, not with excuses, but with "here I am, send me" .

Talk about excuses. Did you know that most flat tires happen on Monday and Fridays, more people are sick on Monday's and Fridays? Could it be that perhaps the selfish desire of a long weekend motivated both? Just asking.

I'm busy, it'll be difficult, I don't deserve it, too old-too young, I'm not strong enough, it'll take a long time, not enough money, every action is a choice, it's about choosing, not excusing.

All excuses are misalignments with the truth of what God says. You've been made more than conquerors, you are well able, you are above and not beneath, the fruit of the spirit is self-control, you are created in the image of God. For too long we've believed a lie, we've believed our excuses. Now is the day to replace those lies with truth applied, not in our minds alone but in our hearts, our souls, and ultimately in our bodies.

Never underestimate your power to change yourself, the spirit of God lives in you so you have all power to change into His image, to become more like Him.

When you correct your mind, everything else will fall into place.

People have excuses for anything that they don't really want to do. Think of church attendance for a moment, what excuses have you heard as to why people don't go? Here's a cute little solution I ran across, it speaks volumes!

One Pastor's Solution: NO EXCUSE SUNDAY: DEDICATED TO MISSING CHURCH ATTENDEES!

"To make it possible for everyone to attend church this Sunday, we are going to have a special "No Excuse Sunday": Cots will be placed in the foyer for those who say, "Sunday is my only day to sleep in". There will be a special section with lounge chairs for those who feel that our pews are too hard. Eye drops will be available for those with tired eyes from watching TV late Saturday nite. We will have steel helmets for those who say, "The roof would cave in if I ever came to church". Blankets will be furnished for those who think the church is too cold, and fans for those who say it is too hot. Score cards will be available for those who wish to list the hypocrites present. Relatives and friends will be in attendance for those who can't go to church and cook dinner, too. We will distribute "Stamp Out Stewardship" buttons for those that feel the church is always asking for money. One section will be devoted to trees and grass for those who like to seek god in nature. Doctors and nurses will be in attendance for those who plan to be sick on Sunday. The sanctuary will be decorated with both Christmas poinsettias and Easter lilies for those who never have seen the church without them. We will provide hearing aids for those who can't hear the preacher and cotton wool for those who think he's too loud! Hope to see you there!

In conclusion, an excuse is simply a way of politely saying, "I don't want to", nothing more and nothing less. No excuses, only surrender! It's time to grow up in all things, including taking responsibility for our behaviours and no longer making excuses so we can get out of doing what we need to do.

Let me give you a brief summary...Excuses are no more than selfish, base desires in response to anything that you don't want to do. It has nothing to do with ability but everything to do with your will. Excuses operate in the Soul (mind, will emotions) All three are involved together to create an excuse. Recognizing an excuse for what it is, is the first step to freeing yourself from the bondage to sin that Paul talks about in Romans 7 & 8.

So I think you've now got a good understanding of excuses, right? Not making excuses but rather submitting to God's power within you and taking responsibility for yourself. That way excuses are not needed, you want to do what God asks of you.

An excuse is worse than a lie, for an excuse is a lie, guarded. Excuses are the tools of incompetence used to build monuments of nothingness

We may stumble but we will not fall; our struggle is not against flesh and blood but against principalities, powers of darkness and rulers in heavenly places. We walk step by step and devour our will one bite at a time. Our choices are made one choice at a time; with consistency and perseverance we will overcome our flesh. ONE BITE AT A TIME.

HOMEWORK: On a piece of paper, split in half, on one side, make a list of all of the excuses that you've given yourself for neglecting your body. On the other side, search for scriptures that speak the truth into each one of the lies that you've been telling yourself.

MY EXCUSES	WHAT GOD SAYS
Eg. I just get anxious, so I eat	**1 Peter 5:6-7** *Humble yourselves, therefore, under the mighty hand of God so that at the proper time he may exalt you, casting all your anxieties on him, because he cares for you.*
Excuse:	God says:
Excuse:	God says:
Excuse:	God says:
Excuse:	God says:

Excuse:	God says:
Excuse:	God says:
Excuse:	God says:

success

obstacles are those
frightful things you see
when you take your
eyes off your goal.

- Henry Ford

WEEK #2

GOAL SETTING

"Where there is no prophetic vision the people cast off restraint, but blessed is the one who heeds wisdom's instruction" (Prov 29:18).

After determining that excuses do not serve our higher purpose, so we must surrender them up, we're now in a position to set goals that are Specific, Measurable, Accountable, Reasonable, Timely and lastly, Sustainable; **SMARTS**. This well-known acronym, less the last 'S', has many meanings but for our purposes the meaning is clear; we want to set goals that are inspired by the Holy Spirit, uniquely designed for each one of us that are not only attainable but can be sustained for a lifetime.

SPECIFIC: Ask the Lord for a target weight that He desires for you, not what a chart says.

MEASURABLE: Scale, measurements or tight pants

31

ACCOUNTABLE: Accountability to participate in weekly sessions; team up with a partner who will keep you accountable while you are learning new habits. Pray for each other as the Holy Spirit leads.

REASONABLE: Check with your leader, accountability partner, and/ or doctor that your goals are reasonable.

TIMELY: Set a date(s) for your goals, perhaps incremental goals, and/or final goal.

SUSTAINABLE: Design a lifestyle that is sustainable given your daily demands.

Goals are intended to bring freedom, not bondage. Therefore goals and planning are flexible and there is no condemnation for not reaching a goal by a specific date. Commitment with perseverance will lead to your goals. God is love and lovingly, through His immeasurable kindness He will lead you to accomplish your goals for Him.

Now that you know the first steps to freedom it's up to you to faithfully walk them out over the next week. If you mess up, simply repent in that moment and turn immediately back to the Lord and His plan for your life's appetites.

"Brothers, I do not consider that I have made it my own. But one thing I do: forgetting what lies behind and straining forward to what lies ahead, I press on toward the goal for the prize of the upward call of God in Christ Jesus" (Phil 3:13-14).

"And the Lord answered me: "Write the vision; make it plain on tablets, so he may run who reads it. For still the vision awaits its appointed time; it hastens to the end—it will not lie. If it seems slow, wait for it; it will surely come; it will not delay." (Hab 2:2-3)

32

"Delight yourself in the Lord, and he will give you the desires of your heart" (Ps 37:4)

"I press on toward the goal for the prize of the upward call of God in Christ Jesus" (Phil 3:14)

"For which of you, desiring to build a tower, does not first sit down and count the cost, whether he has enough to complete it?" (Lk 14:28)

"I can do all things through him who strengthens me" (Ph 4:13)

Trust in the Lord with all your heart, and do not lean on your own understanding. In all your ways acknowledge him, and he will make straight your paths" (Pr 3:5-6)

Finally, brothers, whatever is true, whatever is honorable, whatever is just, whatever is pure, whatever is lovely, whatever is commendable, if there is any excellence, if there is anything worthy of praise, think about these things" (Phil 4:8)

"Jesus said to them, "My food is to do the will of him who sent me and to accomplish his work" (Jn 4:34)

"But grow in the grace and knowledge of our Lord and Savior Jesus Christ. To him be the glory both now and to the day of eternity. Amen" (2 Pet 3:18)

"Enlarge the place of your tent, and let the curtains of your habitations be stretched out; do not hold back; lengthen your cords and strengthen your stakes" (Isa 54:2)

"Where there is no prophetic vision the people cast off restraint, but blessed is he who keeps the law" (Pr 29:18)

"Do not labor for the food that perishes, but for the food that endures to eternal life, which the Son of Man will give

to you. For on him God the Father has set his seal." (Jn 6:27)

"But Jesus looked at them and said, "With man this is impossible, but with God all things are possible." (Mt 19:26)

"For a dream comes with much business, and a fool's voice with many words" (Eccl 5:3)

"Therefore, since we are surrounded by so great a cloud of witnesses, let us also lay aside every weight, and sin which clings so closely, and let us run with endurance the race that is set before us, looking to Jesus, the founder and perfecter of our faith, who for the joy that was set before him endured the cross, despising the shame, and is seated at the right hand of the throne of God. Consider him who endured from sinners such hostility against himself, so that you may not grow weary or fainthearted" (Heb 12:1-3)

"A desire fulfilled is sweet to the soul, but to turn away from evil is an abomination to fools" (Prov 13:19)

He said to them, "Because of your little faith. For truly, I say to you, if you have faith like a grain of mustard seed, you will say to this mountain, 'Move from here to there,' and it will move, and nothing will be impossible for you." (Mt 17:20)

"But seek first the kingdom of God and his righteousness, and all these things will be added to you." (Mt 6:33)

"And whatever you ask in prayer, you will receive, if you have faith." (Mt 21:22)

"So whether we are at home or away, we make it our aim to please him" (2 Cor 5:9)

"You adulterous people! Do you not know that friendship with the world is enmity with God? Therefore whoever wishes to be a friend of the world makes himself an enemy of God". (James 4:4)

"If you turn back your foot from the Sabbath, from doing your pleasure on my holy day, and call the Sabbath a delight and the holy day of the Lord honorable; if you honor it, not going your own ways, or seeking your own pleasure, or talking idly; then you shall take delight in the Lord, and I will make you ride on the heights of the earth; I will feed you with the heritage of Jacob your father, for the mouth of the Lord has spoken." (Isa 58: 13-14)

HOMEWORK: GOAL SETTING This week's homework is to create a Vision Board.

"Look straight ahead, and fix your eyes on what lies before you" (Prov 4:25)

Create a Vision Board, pictures and/or symbols of your goals. Take a regular piece of paper or get creative with Bristol board, paste, colour, use symbols, words or whatever inspires you. Your vision board must represent the place where you want to be. Do not post your "fat pictures" or pictures, words or symbols of what you don't want. We will naturally progress towards what we focus on, that's why when you're driving you need to focus on the road, if you start sight-seeing you'll slowly veer off the road because you head towards what you focus on.

My dad, a great man of God was a concrete truck driver by trade. On Sunday afternoon we would go for a drive in the country-side. I loved the hills and the dropping feeling in my stomach as we rolled over them. Sometimes the drives were a frightening experience because of my dad's sightseeing. He was so excited to show us kids everything, every place where he poured concrete. Once we were driving on a country road on a beautiful sunny day and way in the distance he spotted a magnificent building in the distance, pointing he said, "I poured concrete for that building". It was always exciting to me to see what my dad did but at the moment of his pointing the car veered off the road and my dad took out someone's mailbox as it came smashing into the side of the car at my window. That was scary, and on behalf of my dad I'm sorry if it was your mailbox. My dad didn't even notice, he just kept on driving.

WEEK #3 PORTION DISTORTION

"Honest weights and balances belong to the Lord; he sets the standards for fairness". (Prov 16:11). "A false balance is an abomination to the Lord: but a just weight is his delight" (Prov 11:1)

When learning how much to eat it's often a good idea to choose a child's serving size or eat only half of an adult serving, especially in restaurants. You can ask for a take-out container when you order and then you'll have your lunch for the next day, or you can split the meal with the person beside you, a two for one price special. Make a fist and look at the size of it, your stomach at rest is really only about the size of your fist, feeding a portion of food about that size is very close to what your body needs. Over feeding your stomach will stretch it and cause you to crave more food just to fill the stretched out space. Over drinking, over chewing, over anything is not balance. Use the usual tips of serving your food on a smaller plate, sipping water during your meal or perhaps a glass of water or warm broth before your meal. When you eat, it's important to be thankful and ask the Lord to bless your food prior to consuming it. Recent research on cellular memory seems to indicate that we have may have the power to bless or curse through our language any living material item. Aside from the fact that God is so good to us to give us food, our gratitude and blessing of the food may actually improve the molecular structure in a minute way. If that's not a good enough reason, then Jesus' example of blessing the bread before He broke it to feed the multitudes should be reason enough to pray before you eat.

Keep your meal times pleasant, with uplifting conversation, encouragement and love. *"It's better to have a dry morsel where love is than a house full of feasting with strife" (Prov 17:1)* Not only does pleasant conversation make meal time more enjoyable it also reduces stress, whereas stressful meal times increase cortisol levels which are linked to weight gain.

Re-stock your pantry with healthy foods and eliminate or greatly reduce unhealthy options. If you know that certain foods are a temptation for you; if at all possible remove them from your home. Maybe ice-cream in the home is too much temptation, but if you go a restaurant for ice-cream you'll only eat one small serving and be satisfied. I definitely eat ice-cream only while I'm out, I know that portion control is very difficult when ice-cream is in the home. I did discover the root of my ice-cream cravings when I feel anxious, angry, stressed or even tired. As a small child, my mother would take me for a walk to Dairy Queen every-time she became frustrated with my father. Unknowingly I was learning to associate ice-cream with stress relief. Once I discovered the reason for my cravings I've been able to put ice-cream in its proper place. I actually have a couple of litres of ice-cream in the freezer right now and am not tempted but that's because it's not my favourite kind.

Regular meal times are usually better than one big meal per day, it maintains a balanced blood sugar so you avoid dips and spikes. Breakfast although important, is not mandatory, if you really don't feel like eating first thing in the morning, you can wait a bit, but don't wait until your famished because you'll most likely eat too much. Eating with utensils and putting utensils down between bites slows down your eating to give your brain the opportunity to register fullness which can easily take about 20 minutes after you've had enough to eat. Have your meal at the table then changing location afterwards, ending a meal with a regular routine, like brushing your teeth with minty toothpaste, a cup of tea and/or short devotional practice are all significant ways to establish new routines that signal the end of a meal and will encourage God focus which will help you let go of your excess pounds.

HOMEWORK Journal for 7days Record your food consumption honestly. Did you eat within the boundaries that God gave you? Boundaries may include measuring your portion sizes for those who have severely disordered eating as well as recognizing God's Hunger/Fullness signals? Ultimately, you'll learn to listen to the Lord through the biological signals that He's given you of knowing what, when and how much your body needs of any nutrient.

It is not necessary to eat at all of these occasions. If you're hungry for breakfast, eat it, if not, don't. There are no rules, no laws except for listening to what the Lord has spoken to you specifically. Ask Him what is best for you and eat within those boundaries, then put a check-mark in the Boundary column for every-time you successfully ate within your God given boundaries. Put an **?** for every-time you ate more or not the foods that your body needed. When you see "**?**" ask God why, He'll reveal so He can heal.

This is merely an exercise, not intended to become a focus, or a lifelong habit, that would be way too much focus on the natural, but for learning purposes it's an important step in your spiritual freedom

DAY ONE

DAY #1 TIME	EATING	ATE WITHIN BOUNDARY
	Breakfast:	
	AM Snack:	
	Lunch:	
	PM Snack:	
	Dinner:	
	Evening Snack:	

DAY TWO

DAY #2 TIME	EATING	ATE WITHIN BOUNDARY
	Breakfast:	
	AM Snack:	
	Lunch:	
	PM Snack:	
	Dinner:	
	Evening Snack:	

DAY THREE

DAY #3 TIME	EATING	ATE WITHIN BOUNDARY
	Breakfast:	
	AM Snack:	
	Lunch:	
	PM Snack:	
	Dinner:	
	Evening Snack:	

DAY FOUR

DAY #4 TIME	EATING	ATE WITHIN BOUNDARY
	Breakfast:	
	AM Snack:	
	Lunch:	
	PM Snack:	
	Dinner:	
	Evening Snack:	

DAY FIVE

DAY #5 TIME	EATING	ATE WITHIN BOUNDARY
	Breakfast:	
	AM Snack:	
	Lunch:	
	PM Snack:	
	Dinner:	
	Evening Snack:	

DAY SIX

DAY #6 TIME	EATING	ATE WITHIN BOUNDARY
	Breakfast:	
	AM Snack:	
	Lunch:	
	PM Snack:	
	Dinner:	
	Evening Snack:	

DAY SEVEN

DAY #7 TIME	EATING	ATE WITHIN BOUNDARY
	Breakfast:	
	AM Snack:	
	Lunch:	
	PM Snack:	
	Dinner:	
	Evening Snack:	

WEEK #4
GARDENING:

PULLING OUT
ROOTS OF
OVERINDULGENCE

"You shall not make for yourself any carved image, or any likeness of anything that is in heaven above, or that is in the earth beneath, or that is in the water under the earth; you shall not bow down to them nor serve them. For I, the Lord your God, am a jealous God, visiting the iniquity of the fathers on the children to the third and fourth generations of those who hate Me, but showing mercy to thousands, to those who love Me and keep My commandments." (Exodus 20:4-6)

Gardening was never my area of expertise. Years ago, I had a cute little flower bed in front of my house. One spring day, the pastor's wife was riding by on her bicycle and just stopped in for a quick "hello", she looked at my beautiful flowers in various stages of growth and said, "why do you have potatoes growing in your flower garden?" She could spot potatoes, knew weeds, and knew which plants were flowers. I thought that was amazing since none of the plants had begun to bloom yet. Apparently, I didn't know the difference between potatoes, weeds or flowers. Today, there are many of us who do not know the difference between what is the desired plant and what is the weed.

We listen to the rules and regulations of eating or living and say, I must do this, or I must do that, then we design for ourselves a law or set of self-righteous rules just like the Pharisees did. God is not glorified through legalism; He is glorified through obedience to Him which is much simpler if we choose to listen and are willing to deny ourselves.

Unfortunately some of us have been born into families where generations before us have believed and acted upon lies or upon man made rules for living. This is what we call a generational curse, and this is what we will root out and destroy, so that we can bring forth good fruit.

Today, we're going to do a bit of gardening while the ground is soft and the plants are not fully developed we can till the ground, pluck out the weeds and give the plant the most fertile ground for growth. We're going to eliminate three things: greed, need, and weeds from our garden. These three things are about to leave your life as you eliminate all envy, jealousy and strife from your life. Again, there are some roots and weeds that are very deep, and require interventions that are beyond this course. Please seek out that intervention through your pastor or spiritual leader who can best advise you.

On the note of demons and curses, don't let that scare you in any way. In the 10 Commandments God speaks, *"You must not make for yourself an idol of any kind or an image of anything in the heavens or on the earth or in the sea. You must not bow down to them or worship them, for I, the Lord your God, am a jealous God who will not tolerate your affection for any other gods. I lay the sins of the parents upon their children; the entire family is affected—even children in the third and fourth generations of those who reject me. But I lavish unfailing love for a thousand generations on those who love me and obey my commands"* (Ex 20:6)

An idol is anything that you worship, the object of your affection. That might be a material possession or another person or perhaps even the food on your plate. Just think of it for a moment, how much time do you spend thinking about food, watching cooking shows or thumbing through recipe books, planning what to eat, preparing food, and even taking pictures of food. The pictures are beautiful, mouth watering, they stimulate the appetite and increase cravings; they idolize the creation, hungering for the taste and glorying in the presentation of dishes. Now, not to become off-balanced, a beautiful well prepared meal for the purpose of blessing your family or guests, is a gift of love to them. But if the truth be told, there are times that what is really occurring is a gift to your flesh, not a gift from your spirit. It's more of a secret rendezvous with your idol, your love, your pizza, ice-cream, (beer, coffee, chocolate, cigarettes) or whatever you consume in excess or in secret.

Don't become frightened or think that you are hopeless because your family is riddled with various abuses, addictions and idolatry. You may have some dirt in your family line, but you also may have a praying great, great, great grandma who served God with her whole heart. Her blessings also were passed down to you. Or maybe you are a first generation Kingdom citizen, demons can only remain with your permission. Knowledge is power, the Truth will set you free.

The price has been paid in full by Jesus' blood, so we are no longer under the curse of sin and death. The curse we feel that we are experiencing is simply a demon who attached to us to taunt, provoke or invade our space because we unknowingly have given an open door in our lives. We'll look at how some of those doors opened, have you confess any participation with darkness, then ask you to pray alone or with someone to renounce any participation with the sin, habit, addiction or fear that binds us, and repent of any specific sins, finally we'll declare our freedom from the curse. We can no longer be cursed because Jesus lives within us, *"The Lord his God is with him, and the shout of king is among them" (Num 23:21)*

It's up to us to keep the door to sin closed by not participating in the thoughts and behaviours that lead to opening doors of darkness.

The bottom line is to repent for yielding to the temptation of lust for food. *"Whose end is destruction, whose God is their belly, and whose glory is in their shame, who mind earthly things." (Phil 3:19)* After repentance, ask the Lord for the power to overcome your poor eating choices or gluttony and resist the devil through relationship and obedience to God. *"Submit yourselves therefore to God. Resist the devil, and he will flee from you." (James 4:7)*

You're mounting a comeback, you may have been knocked down but just like BoBo the punching clown, you may have been knocked down but you're coming back. You can't be defeated in the Lord. In Him alone there is ALWAYS Victory! You are recovering all of your spiritual strength as you let go of your ego, your control, your ways for the Kingdom Weigh (way). Just as David, you'll recover your strength of character...; ...discernment; ...love, ...wisdom; ...prayer; ...integrity; and strength of faith.

 "Ye shall not need to fight in this battle: set yourselves, stand ye still, and see the salvation of the Lord with you." (II Chronicles 20:17)

HOMEWORK: Breaking Free of Generational Curses, Habits, Addictions & Fears

Generational Sins: Highlight any of the categories below that may be involved with your issues today; either you or those before you going back up to 3-4 generations may have struggled with it.

Spiritually opened doors: This List is commonly used to identify possible spiritual doors that have been opened allowing the enemy to work evil in your life. In some cases the sin pattern is not recognized, or has become a stronghold that requires deliverance at a deeper level than what is intended within this teaching. This teaching is for the purpose of self evaluation, confession, repentance and commitment to walk in God's way.

Please identify the sin patterns that your ancestors, and/or you, are involved with that relates to your disordered eating.

Indicate with an 'S' (self) if it applies to you directly and an 'A' (ancestors) if it applies to your parents, grandparents, and/or your great grandparents in the spaces provided.

When you pray to break these generational curses you may pray alone or seek out a trusted, mature partner to pray with you. The issues that are Strongly Related to your Issue are the ones that must be prayed through, others as the Lord leads.

Examples: _A S_ (Strongly Related to My Issue)

(Note: in the examples, both **Ancestors** and 'Self' were involved in these sins.)

___ ___ Abandonment	___ ___ Chronic Illness
___ ___ Demonic Torment	___ ___ Idolatry
___ ___ Occult Involvement	
	___ ___ Strife/Division
___ ___ Abuse Emotional	

___ ___ Depression/ Grief	___ ___ Confusion
___ ___ Parents/In-Law Issues	___ ___ Job Related Issues
	___ ___Suicide Thoughts/ Attempts
___ ___ Abuse Physical	___ ___ Communication, Little or Poor
___ ___ Divorce/Separation	___ ___ Lack of Intimacy
___ ___ Perfectionism	___ ___ Trauma
___ ___ Abuse Sexual	___ ___Control Issues
___ ___ Drugs, Legal/ Illegal	_____Legal Issues/ Problems
___ ___ Post-Traumatic Stress	___ ___ Unbelief/Doubt
_____Abuse Spiritual	___ ___ Cult Involvement
	___ ___Loss
_____Emotional Abandonment	___ ___ Unfulfilled Lives
___ ___ Premarital Issues	___ ___ Cutting
___ ___ Abuse Verbal	___ ___ Marriage Issues
___ ___ Failure	___ ___ Unforgiveness
___ ___ Pride	___ ___ Cyber Sex
___ ___ Addictions/ Compulsions	___ ___ Neglect
	_____Unworthiness/ Inferiority
___ ___ Family Secrets	___ ___ Death, Premature Death
___ ___ Rebellion	

___ ___ Anxiety	___ ___ Mental Illness
___ ___ Favoritism	_____Victimization/ Passivity
___ ___ Rejection	___ ___ Deception/Lying
___ ___ Anorexia/Bulimia	___ ___ New Age/Gothic
___ ___ Fears/Anxiety	___ ___ Violence
_____Religious Issues/ Legalism	___ ___ Deceptive Business Practices
___ ___ Anger/Rage	_____Not Wanted/Outsider
_____Financial Issues/Problems	___ ___ Withdrawal
_____Sexual Bondage / Issues	
_____Bitterness/ Criticalness	
___ ___ Freemasonry	
___ ___ Shame/Guilt	
___ ___ Bound/Hindered Emotions	
___ ___ Gender Identity Confusion	
___ ___ Sleep Problems	

Ungodly beliefs about myself

Read the following statements that you believe and mark (**X**) the ones that **directly relate** to your current issue. Here we are <u>looking for themes.</u> There are likely some categories that are more prevalent than others, focus on renouncing the lie that you've believed and replace it with the truth. Renouncing the lie without replacing the truth is like cleaning the house of demons but not sealing the door with truth, giving an opening for more demonic influence to enter. casting_out_dem dy

"Submit yourselves therefore to God. Resist the devil, and he will flee from you". (James 4:7)

"When the unclean spirit has gone out of a person, it passes through waterless places seeking rest, but finds none. Then it says, 'I will return to my house from which I came.' And when it comes, it finds the house empty, swept, and put in order. Then it goes and brings with it seven other spirits more evil than itself, and they enter and dwell there, and the last state of that person is worse than the first. So also will it be with this evil generation." (Mt 12: 43-45)

"Finally, be strong in the Lord and in the strength of his might. Put on the whole armor of God, that you may be able to stand against the schemes of the devil. For we do not wrestle against flesh and blood, but against the rulers, against the authorities, against the cosmic powers over this present darkness, against the spiritual forces of evil in the heavenly places. Therefore take up the whole armor of God, that you may be able to withstand in the evil day, and having done all, to stand firm. Stand therefore, having fastened on the belt of truth, and having put on the breastplate of righteousness" (Eph 6: 10-18)

"Be sober-minded; be watchful. Your adversary the devil prowls around like a roaring lion, seeking someone to devour." (1 Pet 5:8)

Theme: Rejection, Not Belonging

____ 1. I don't belong. I will always be on the outside (left out).

____ 2. My feelings don't count. No one cares what I feel.

____ 3. No one will love me or care about me just for myself.

____ 4. I will always be lonely. The special man (woman) in my life will not be there for me.

Theme: Unworthiness, Guilt, Shame

____ 1. I am not worthy to receive anything from God.

____ 2. I am the problem. When something is wrong, it is my fault.

____ 3. I am a bad person. If you knew the real me, you would reject me.

____ 4. If I wear a mask, people won't find out how horrible I am and reject me.

____ 5. I have messed up so badly that I have missed God's best for me.

Theme: Doing to achieve Self worth, Value, Recognition

____ 1. I will never get credit for what I do.

____ 2. My value is in what I do. I am valuable because I do good to others or because I am 'successful.'

___ 3. Even when I do or give my best, it is not good enough. I can never meet the standard.

___ 4. God doesn't care if I have a 'secret life,' as long as I appear to be good.

Theme: Control (to avoid hurt)

___ 1. I have to plan every day of my life. I have to continually plan/strategize. I can't relax.

___ 2. The perfect life is one in which no conflict is allowed and so there is peace.

___ 3. I can avoid conflict that would risk losing others' approval by being passive and not do anything.

___ 4. The best way to avoid more hurt, rejection, etc., is to isolate myself.

Theme: Physical

___ 1. I am unattractive. God shortchanged me.

___ 2. I am doomed to have certain physical disabilities. They are just part of what I have inherited.

Theme: Personality Traits

___ 1. I will always be _____ (angry, shy, jealous, insecure, fearful, etc.).

___ 2. I will never be _____ (likable, lovable, happy, safe, content, etc.).

Theme: Identity

___ 1. I should have been a boy (girl), then my parents would have valued/loved me more ..., etc.

___ 2. Men (women) have it better.

___ 3. I will never be known or appreciated for my real self.

___ 4. I will never really change and be as God wants me to be.

___ 5. I am not competent/complete as a man (woman).

Theme: Miscellaneous

___ 1. I have wasted a lot of time and energy, some of my best years.

___ 2. Turmoil is normal for me.

___ 3. I will always have financial problems.

Ungodly Beliefs about Others

Theme: Safety/Protection

___ 1. I must be very guarded about what I say since anything I say may be used against me.

___ 2. I have to guard and hide my emotions and feelings.

___ 3. I cannot give anyone the satisfaction of knowing that they have wounded or hurt me. I'll not be vulnerable, humiliated, or shamed.

___ 4. The best way to survive is to (___avoid, ___overpower) other people.

___ 5. I will always need to be strong in order to protect and defend myself.

___ 6. It's not safe to submit myself to anyone.

Theme: Retaliation

____ 1. The correct way to respond if someone offends me is to punish them by withdrawing and/or

cutting them off.

____ 2. I will make sure that _____ hurts as much as I do!

Theme: Victim

____ 1. Authority figures will humiliate me and violate me.

____ 2. I will always be used and abused by other people.

____ 3. My value is based totally on others' judgment/perception about me.

____ 4. I am completely under their authority. I have no will or choice of my own.

____ 5. I will not be known, understood, loved, or appreciated for who I am by those close to me.

____ 6. The significant people in my life are not there for me and will not be there for me when I need them.

Theme: Hopelessness/Helplessness

____ 1. I am out there all alone. If I get into trouble or need help, there is no one to rescue me.

____ 2. I have made such a mess of my life there is no use going on.

____ 3. I am a victim of my circumstances and there is no hope for change.

____ 4. I'm all alone.

___ 5. Something is wrong with me.

Theme: Defective in Relationships

___ 1. I will never be able to fully give or receive love. I don't know what it is.

___ 2. If I let anyone get close to me, I may get my heart broken again. I can't let myself risk it.

___ 3. If I fail to please you, I won't receive your pleasure and acceptance of me.

___ 4. I must strive (perfectionism) to do whatever is necessary to try to please you.

___ 5. I will never be a priority with those in authority over me.

Theme: God

___ 1. God loves other people more than He loves me.

___ 2. God only values me for what I do. My life is just a means to an end.

___ 3. No matter how much I try, I'll never be able to do enough nor do it well enough to please God.

___ 4. God is judging me when I relax. I have to stay busy about His work or He will punish me.

___ 5. God has let me down before. He may do it again. I can't trust Him or feel secure with Him.

The purpose of this exercise is to bring these sins before the Father, confess them, and then speak the truth of what God says over yourself. Get into a place of worship, then sit quietly before the Lord and pray in your own words, something like:

PRAYER: Father God, I come before you, hungering for more of you, but these sins from my past seem to haunt me, I struggle with the sins of the past. I thank-you that you have set me free from my past, and so even now, I confess…., I renounce any participation with these lies (name each one) that I've believed about myself, my family, others, even you. *"Create in me a clean heart, O God, and renew a right spirit within me. Cast me not away from your presence, and take not your Holy Spirit from me. Restore to me the joy of your salvation, and uphold me with a willing spirit. Then I will teach transgressors your ways, and sinners will return to you." (Ps 51: 10-13)* AMEN!

WEEK #5

THE BEST FOOD – PHYSICAL EATING PLANS

– Spiritual Nutrition *"My nourishment comes from doing the will of God, who sent me, and from finishing his work. (John 4:34)*

"So don't let anyone condemn you for what you eat or drink, or for not celebrating certain holy days or new moon ceremonies or Sabbaths. For these rules are only shadows of the reality yet to come. And Christ himself is that reality". *(Col 2: 16-17)*

Now it's time to ask for God's plan for your weight loss. Allow Him to lead you as to what He wants you to do. He knows your body and He will direct you as to how you are to eat. Ask for a desire for healthy foods and ask Him to remove your cravings for unhealthy foods. *"And this is the confidence that we have in him, that, if we ask any thing according to his will, he hears us: And if we know that he hear us, whatsoever we ask, we know that we have the petitions that we desired of him."* *(1 John 5:14-15)*

Our focus must be on the Lord throughout this process of learning or relearning balance, not on eat this--don't eat that. We are drawn to what we focus on. Today in society almost 1/3 of all adults at any one time are focusing on some diet. In fact many today are literally dying because of it. Over the past 50 years that focus on diet, exercise, physical health has exponentially increased, yet we've grown more and more unhealthy with a major increase in

61

lifestyle diseases such as diabetes (type 2), stroke, osteoporosis, some cancers, and heart disease etc. What would life be like if 1/3 were wholly focused on knowing God?

Diets get pretty confusing, do this, don't do that, and next week on the news, facebook or somewhere popping up in your face the experts are saying to do something different. God desires balance and moderation. He already gave us the perfect portion size gauge housed in the hypothalamus within our brain. It tells us when we're hungry or thirsty, when it's time to eat or drink, it also tells us when we've had enough food, unfortunately, as a rebellious people we don't always listen. Today, we want to begin to listen attentively to what the Holy Spirit is saying to us. He speaks in many different ways; one of those ways is through our biological design of hunger and fullness, as the exercises that you did in week two. He also shows us what foods our body needs, through our appetite if our appetite is not distorted from years of neglect and abuse. Through listening to the voice of the Lord, and careful attention to how he speaks to us we can relearn what our bodies are asking for. So don't despair if you've abused your body, it's not the past that God is concerned about, it's your future. He has great plans for your future, today is the day to start walking that out for His glory. Simply confess your sin of neglect, abuse and anything else that you've done to yourself that did not come from a place of Love, for God is love so we need to start treating ourselves with love from the inside out.

There is much discussion and discrepancy between eating plans, some are merely created for the sake of profit and others through scientific research. Some are based on geographical criteria or cultural preferences.

I propose to you that there is not one plan that suits all, that we are all uniquely created and that given a wide variety of foods we will naturally choose the foods that our bodies require in the quantity that it requires if we have not become desensitized to the voice of the Lord in our eating habits due to years of casting off restraint, greed and idolatry. Fortunately, through God's grace this can change now. I've got a few popular nutritional plans below, each of them has some validity but the final decision is between you and the Lord. No longer will gluttonous behaviour be on your agenda, but rather giving of thanks and moderation in all of your eating behaviours.

You may choose to use Canada's food guide as a basic nutritional guideline, or stay closer to a Vegetarian, Vegan, Paleo, or Low Carb nutritional approach. Just consult with the Lord, use wisdom and research if in question of how to live any of these mentioned lifestyles in a healthy way. Your body does require all 3 macro-nutrients, Fat, Carbohydrate and Protein, but in different ratios and from different sources for different people. Learn your ratios by starting to listen to your body and how it feels after eating certain foods. If the foods cause an adverse reaction, perhaps sluggishness then maybe a different food choice or eating plan might suit you better. It's not complicated or scary, it's simply a matter of tuning in to the Lord and hearing what He is saying to you. If you hear the Lord say to eat only bacon, let's say, then it would be wise to consult with someone who has the mind of the Lord and they will guide you into a healthier eating plan that is more balanced.

"Hear thou, my son, and be wise, and guide thine heart in the way. Be not among winebibbers; among riotous eaters of flesh: For the drunkard and the glutton shall come to poverty: and drowsiness shall clothe a man with rags." (Prov 23:19-21)

"Let your moderation be known unto all men. The Lord is at hand" (Phil 4:5)

"For bodily exercise profiteth little: but godliness is profitable unto all things, having promise of the life that now is, and of that which is to come" (1 Timothy 4:8)

"Please test your servants for ten days, and let us be given some vegetables to eat and water to drink (Daniel 1:12-17) This is a fast, not a nutritional lifestyle.

As the Book of Acts makes clear, Christians are not obligated to follow the eating laws of the old testament. This is made clear in Peter's vision in Acts 10:15. Peter saw a vision of a sheet come down with unclean animals and is told, *"What God has made clean, do not call common."* In other words, there is no kosher code for Christians. Christians are not concerned with eating kosher foods and avoiding all others. That part of the law is no longer binding, and Christians can enjoy shrimp and pork with no injury to conscience although the word also says that all things are allowed --but not everything is good for you. Eating a chocolate bar for dinner is allowed but it's not the best nutrition, so wisdom, listening to the Lord would direct you to balanced eating.

Compare & Discuss: Today, there is so much focus on weight loss, eat this--don't eat that. Eat as this time, eat it raw--cook it fully, don't eat fruit and vegetables together, buy organic—organic is not worth the label, don't eat fruit alone, must eat within 1 hour of waking up, must not eat 3 hours before sleep, must It's a trap of legalism that's as deadly as the trap of Pharmaceutical Industry.

All of these rules and regulations only promote greater bondage to man's system, not Gods, they steal your time, energy, finances, and can compromise health rather than enhance your life, they become your life, they become an idol and receive their worship.

Weight Loss, and focus on Physical Health is a multi-billion dollar industry in Canada. Can you imagine if only a Tithe of that industry came into God's Kingdom the great work that would be done to transform lives from the inside out?

In Fact this is my Theme Song for Life, "From the Inside Out" by Hillsong United. It's a powerful truth that the change for weight loss is not a diet, nor a formula prescribed by man. The changes in our body come from the inside out. This song is especially encouraging and life giving when it comes to repeated failures, which sometimes becomes the focus when breaking free of dysfunctional eating (life) habits. Did you know that statistically the average person goes on 11 major lifestyle renovations (diets, stop smoking, breaking any addiction cycle) before breaking free.

Take a moment and read (or sing) these words and really meditate upon them; let God make them alive in your spirit, they will transform you!

From the Inside Out

By Hillsong United

A thousand times I've failed
Still Your mercy remains
And should I stumble again
I'm caught in Your grace
Everlasting, Your light will shine when all else fades
Never ending Your glory goes beyond all fame

In my heart and my soul

Lord I give You control
Consume me from the inside out,
Lord, let justice and praise
Become my embrace
To love you from the inside out.

Your will above all else
My purpose remains
The art of losing myself
In bringing You praise
Everlasting
Your light will shine when all else fades
Never ending
Your glory goes beyond all fame

In my heart and my soul
Lord I give You control
Consume me from the inside out,
Lord, let justice and praise
Become my embrace
To love You from the inside out.

Everlasting
Your light will shine when all else fades
Never ending
Your glory goes beyond all fame
And the cry of my heart
Is to bring You praise
From the inside out
Lord my soul cries out

In my heart and my soul
Lord I give you control
Consume me from the inside out,
Lord, let justice and praise
Become my embrace

To love You from the inside out.

Everlasting
Your light will shine when all else fades
Never ending
Your glory goes beyond all fame
And the cry of my heart
Is to bring You praise
From the inside out
Lord my soul cries out.

Everlasting Your light will shine when all else fades
Never ending Your glory goes beyond all fame
And the cry of my heart
Is to bring You praise
From the inside out
Lord my soul cries out

Open your eyes to Truth and the Spirit of Truth will set you
Free!

COMPARISON: Some of today's most popular diets

Canada's Food Guide

 Bible / Rainbow / Genesis Diet

Low Carb / Ketogenic / Paleo

Vegan / Vegetarian

Raw Food Diet

CANADA'S FOOD GUIDE:
Recommended Number of Food Guide Servings per Day

| | Children | | | Teens | | Adults | | | |
| | 2-3 | 4-8 | 9-13 | 14-18 Years | | 19-50 Years | | 51+ Years | |
	Girls and Boys			Female	Male	Female	Male	Female	Male
Vegetables and Fruit	4	5	6	7	8	7-8	8-10	7	7
Grain Products	3	4	6	6	7	6-7	8	6	7
Milk and Alternatives	2	2	3-4	3-4	3-4	2	2	3	3
Meat and Alternatives	1	1	1-2	2	3	2	3	2	3

For example:

If you are a 35 year old woman you should aim to have:

> 7-8 vegetables and fruit
> 6-7 grain products
> 2 milk and alternatives
> 2 meat and alternatives
> 30 - 45 mL (2 to 3 Tbsp) of unsaturated oils and fats

In Canada, the Food Guide undergoes changes from time to time based on research. It is true that some of that research if funded by various boards such as wheat, meat or dairy boards, who perhaps want to promote their own agendas. Whether that is true, or not, there is an alarming increase in obesity and obesity related diseases. Get's you thinkin!

The BIBLE DIET (Also known as Rainbow or Genesis Diet)

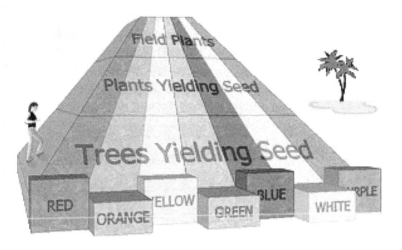

The Bible Diet also called Rainbow Diet or Genesis Diet: scriptures reveal the clean biblical diet foods that form God's healing banquet based at the tree of life.

Acknowledges 4 Bible Food Groups

1. **Trees** that are edible yield is bearing seed or is seeds.
   Examples: apples, avocados, grapefruit, pecans, papaya, cherries, olives
   "I have given you every plant with seeds on the face of the earth and every tree that has fruit with seeds. This will be your food." (Gen 1:29)

2. **Plants** whose edible yield is bearing seed or is seeds. Examples: tomatoes, beans, lentils, wheat, berries, squash, corn, rye

3. **Field plants** herbs, roots, leafy vegetables.
   "He causes the grass to grow for the cattle, and herb for the service of man: that he may bring forth food out of the earth" (Ps 104:14)

4. Clean meat *"You are therefore to make a distinction between the clean animal and the unclean, and between the unclean bird and the clean; and you shall not make yourselves detestable by animal or by bird or by anything that creeps on the ground, which I have separated for you as   unclean."*
(Leviticus 20:25)

The Bible undoubtedly says that we need to be careful not to judge our brothers or sisters for what they eat or do not eat. *"Now accept the one who is weak in faith, but not for the purpose of passing judgment on his opinions. One person has faith that he may eat all things, but he who is weak eats vegetables only. The one who eats is not to regard with contempt the one who does not eat, and the one who does not eat is not to judge the one who eats, for God has accepted him" (Rom 14:1-3)*

Clearly, what one eats is of no concern to the other believer, but love prevails and when you sit with another person honor that person whom Christ died for by not trying to impose your personal convictions on them. If their conscience convicts them, then they should listen to their conscience. *"Therefore, if food causes my brother to stumble, I will never eat meat again, so that I will not cause my brother to stumble" (1 Cor 8:15)*

"Whoever causes one of these little ones who believe in me to sin, it would be better for him if a great millstone were hung around his neck and he were thrown into the sea".(Mark 9:42)

LOW CARB LIFESTYLES (Ketogenic / Paleo)

Low Carb and versions of low carb, Ketogenic , Paleo etc.

All food is made up of three primary macro nutrients – carbohydrates (or sugars), proteins, and fats. Low carb implies that the percentage of carbohydrate (by calorie) is low – but lower than what?

- **High Carb** 50-70% (Canada's Food Guide, Vegan/Vegetarian)
- **Moderate Carb** 40-50% (Most Paleo)
- **Low Carb** 25-39% (Zone, Atkins)
- **Very Low Carb** 0-25% (Ketogenic)

However it is common to find that any diet less than 50-60% carb ratio is called a *low carb diet*. Depending on one's sensitivity to carbohydrates, a moderate carb ratio may be better than a high carb ratio.

In Sweden they have officially incorporated a Low Carb High Fat eating plan as a recommendation for a healthy lifestyle. Fat is the only nutrient that does not affect blood sugar and insulin production. Insulin is the fat storing hormone, so without it you don't store fat. Carbs raise insulin which in turn stores fat, therefore limiting carbohydrate consumption to a level that your body can metabolize makes sense. Excess will cause weight gain. Again, it comes down to listening to the Lord on what nutritional plan works best for you. Many people around the world do very well on high carb nutritional plans where other people, simply do not, but they benefit greatly from a low carb nutritional plan.

A Low Carb or Ketogenic (nutritional ketosis) lifestyle may improve cholesterol levels, reduce triglyceride levels, reduce blood sugar and insulin levels which is a major improvement for type 2 diabetes, reduce high blood pressure, reduce seizures, improve memory and more. *Reminder,* if you take medication for any condition please consult with your physician, failure to do so can have dire consequences, which I discovered the hard way. I was taking two medications for HBP while losing weight. I lost consciousness and was rushed to the hospital via ambulance. The problem was low blood pressure because as a stubborn, unwise individual I did not share with my doctor my weight loss. Had he have known he would have monitored my BP and reduced meds accordingly. From that hospital visit on I've never needed medication again for HBP nor have I struggled with stabilizing my blood sugars. I've never needed medication for that all because of dietary lifestyle changes.

Paleo is a relatively new idea, although claimed to be an ancient way of eating based on hunter/gatherers. It's also called the caveman diet, includes meat, fish, shellfish, eggs, tree nuts, vegetables, roots, fruits, berries, mushrooms etc. The copious amounts of fruits may raise the carb ratio to moderate or even high carb, depending on the individual practicing this nutritional approach, although it totally eliminate grains, dairy, starchy vegetables, sugar and fake foods.

Vegan vs Vegetarian's both do not eat meat. However, while vegetarians tend to consume dairy products and eggs, a vegan avoids *all* animal products, including eggs and dairy, and often inedible animal-based products, such as leather, wool, and silk. Vegetarianism is usually a diet, while veganism is a lifestyle usually rooted in a philosophical belief system. Vegetarians often choose their diet based on its reported health benefits or for religious or political reasons. In general, vegans have much stronger political beliefs regarding their diet, with some believing animals should be protected under many of the same laws that humans are. Vegan or Vegetarian eating plans can be nutritious but extra attention needs to be paid to make sure that that adequate protein and nutrients are taken in. Their macro-nutrient ratio is generally higher in carbohydrates due to the vegetables, fruits and grains. raw fruits, vegetables, and grains.

Raw Food Diets: The idea is that heating food destroys its nutrients and natural enzymes, which is bad because enzymes boost digestion and fight chronic disease. In short: When you cook it, you kill it.

Some raw food dieters believe cooking makes food toxic. They claim that a raw food diet can clear up headaches and allergies, boost immunity and memory, and improve arthritis and diabetes

But there are drawbacks. You have to make sure you're getting enough protein, iron, calcium, and other vitamins and minerals like B12. Because most people who eat raw foods exclude animal products, you may need to take vitamin supplements to make up for any gaps in your diet.

Plus, cooking isn't all bad. It boosts some nutrients, like beta-carotene and lycopene. It also kills bacteria, which helps you avoid food poisoning. And there's no proof that eating only raw foods prevents illness.

Almost all nutritional approaches do agree that eating between hunger and fullness by rating your hunger between 1-10. 1 being famished, 10 being stuffed and eating only between the ranges of 3-7 are fundamental principles of health. Also, they all tend to agree that sugar is not beneficial, in fact sugar stimulates the same neuro-receptors that are activated with cocaine usage. Artificial foods, sweeteners, packaged foods are either not acceptable or to be used sparingly, natural sweeteners are far more beneficial such as honey, agave or even stevia. Lastly, exercise. Moderate exercise is beneficial for a number of reasons including increasing serotonin (the feel good hormone), improving cardiovascular function, building muscle which burns slightly more calories than fat and most of all movement is fun. If you hate gyms, like I do, try dancing before the Lord, or playing a Djembe drum, a walk in nature perhaps? These are my favourite exercises. Discover what you like to do, as you lose weight you'll find that you have more energy and will want to do more, for now, do a little of something that you enjoy. No rules, no laws, just move in step with God.

HOMEWORK: Search out one scripture or story to share with group the revelation of what the Lord is showing you regarding food or eating.

WEEK #6

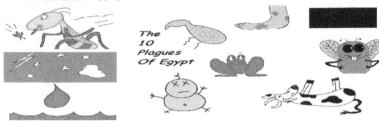

The 10 Plagues Of Egypt

PHAROAH'S CONTROL – 10 PLAGUES OF EGYPT

– 10 Thought patterns that we must overcome to become free; the final battle is the death of the first born, our Adamic nature (sin nature) must die before we enter our promised land—Freedom in Christ

Pharoah is an evil controller that operates within our minds in an attempt to keep us in bondage. Pharoah-Let my people Go!

Exodus 7 This chapter speaks of a spiritual awakening, it's a revelation of alignment of Pharoah (your mind) to the prophet (your heart). An alignment of Pharoah/mind with your Heart as in One in Love; God's greatest desire is that we would become one starting with one within ourselves. We must become one within before we can become one with each other. Unity begins in the Kingdom of our hearts.

In this Exodus story we see Aaron's rod become a serpent and swallow up the magician's rods. All scripture has multi-dimensional interpretation. Historical accounts, future revelation and present truth application. Here we have Aaron's rod that represents the authority of the voice of God within your heart. This prophetic voice takes authority over all other (self/sin/Satan's) voices. It strips the enemy of his authority and that is what we are doing in this teaching. We are using the authority given us through Jesus blood and His gift to us of the Holy Spirit. We're declaring the authority of truth and stripping the enemy of any perceived power that we've allowed him in our lives.

The Exodus is a shadow under the Old Covenant of the Resurrection in the New Covenant. *"But now, by dying to what once bound us, we have been released from the law so that we serve in the new way of the Spirit" Rom 7:6*

So you see, just as death came into the world through a man, now the resurrection from the dead has begun through another man. 1 Cor 15:21

We've been set free from the law of sin and death...READ ROMANS 8

Excerpt from Romans 8 "Consequently, there is now no condemnation for those who are in Christ Jesus. For the law of the Spirit of life in Christ Jesus has set you free from the law of sin and death. For what was impossible for the law, in that it was weak through the flesh, God did. By sending his own Son in the likeness of sinful flesh and concerning sin, he condemned sin in the flesh, in order that the requirement of the law would be fulfilled in us, who do not live according to the flesh but according to the Spirit. For those who are living according to the flesh are intent on the things of the flesh, but those who are living according to the Spirit are intent on the things of the Spirit. For the mindset of the flesh is death, but the mindset of the Spirit is life and peace, because the mindset of the flesh is enmity toward God, for it is not subjected to the law of God, for it is not able to do so, and those who are in the flesh are not able to please God.

But you are not in the flesh but in the Spirit, if indeed the Spirit of God lives in you. But if anyone does not have the

Spirit of Christ, this person does not belong to him" (Rom 8 1-9)

Plague #1: BLOOD Ex 7:15

Polluted river brings death to the fish (river of life flow in us will not bring forth souls for the kingdom if it's polluted). Feeding our minds with lies and evil thoughts pollutes our river...lifeless waters. The polluted water was undrinkable, there was a tremendous thirst in the land that nothing could satisfy from Pharoah's kingdom. Water of the word is unavailable to us due to mental, or physical depletion; it's dry and we thirst for living water but can't find it. (Ps 63) We hunger and thirst after righteousness with an unquenchable thirst that only God can satisfy therefore we must seek God first and His righteousness, any other way is a back door that does not give life eternal or abundant. *"Finally, brothers, whatever is true, whatever is honorable, whatever is just, whatever is pure, whatever is lovely, whatever is commendable, if there is any excellence, if there is anything worthy of praise, think about these things." (Phil 4:8)*

Plague #2: FROGS Ex 8:1

Swarm with frogs is symbolic of the jumping of our thoughts from truth to lies—lies to truth – faith to fear – fear to faith– God's thoughts to self to sin to Satan and back again. *"But when you ask, you must believe and not doubt, because the one who doubts is like a wave of the sea, blown and tossed by the wind. That person should not expect to receive anything from the Lord. Such a person is double-minded and unstable in all they do. It's been proven that man cannot think on two things at exactly the same time, what happens in fact is that they vacillate rapidly from one thought to the other and back again. This is what happens with an unstable mind, just like the jumping frogs they jump from selfish desires, lust or evil thoughts to God, faith and back again...this man is unstable in all his ways. (James 1: 6-8)*

The Lord desires that *"we will no longer be immature like children. We won't be tossed and blown about by every wind of new teaching. We will not be influenced when people try to trick us with lies so clever they sound like the truth. Instead, we will speak the truth in love, growing in every way more and more like Christ, who is the head of his body, the church. He makes the whole body fit together perfectly. As each part does its own special work, it helps the other parts grow, so that the whole body is healthy and growing and full of love. (Eph 4: 14-16)*

A little earlier in this chapter in Ephesians Paul encourages us as prisoners of the Lord to walk worthy of our calling. Every believer has a calling, a rank in the body of Christ, a specific set of gifts and talents. It doesn't matter, what, whether little or lot; it's how we use what God has given us for His glory. He sees the heart; He knows our thoughts and judges righteously. His heart's cry is that we would love each other and become one body fit together with love through humility and gentleness. It's really simple...get addicted...to Jesus...to Love...to the Spirit of the Lord with you, to the Source of all Life...to GOD!

Plague #3 Gnats Ex 8:16

"What sorrow awaits you teachers of religious law and you Pharisees. Hypocrites! For you are careful to tithe even the tiniest income from your herb gardens, but you ignore the more important aspects of the law—justice, mercy, and faith. You should tithe, yes, but do not neglect the more important things. Blind guides! You strain your water so you won't accidentally swallow a gnat, but you swallow a camel! "What sorrow awaits you teachers of religious law

and you Pharisees. Hypocrites! For you are so careful to clean the outside of the cup and the dish, but inside you are filthy—full of greed and self-indulgence! (Mtt 23: 23-25)

Without getting into a theological debate on eternal salvation-- Calvinism vs Arminianism, how about just reading the word of God for yourself, settle it in your heart, and if there is a line where one can cross and lose salvation, let's just not get anywhere near it. It's a dangerous game to play, to say in your heart, maybe just a little sin, maybe just a little..... Many people have said, just a little crack, alcohol, pornography, gambling, etc. and found themselves opening a door to a nightmare of bondage. Let's choose to cleave to the Lord in all things at all times and rest in Him securely with a pure conscience, *a pure heart for to those with a pure heart are blessed, for they will see God (Mtt 5:8).*

"Not everyone who calls out to me, 'Lord! Lord!' will enter the Kingdom of Heaven. Only those who actually do the will of my Father in heaven will enter. On judgment day many will say to me, 'Lord! Lord! We prophesied in your name and cast out demons in your name and performed many miracles in your name.' But I will reply, 'I never knew you. Get away from me, you who break God's laws.' (Mtt 7:24-27)

Plague #4 Swarms of Flies Ex 20

Flies carry all sorts of bacteria and feast on decay and rotten flesh. Our negative mindsets, complaining, doubt and unbelief bring rottenness to our flesh and attract the swarms of flies to our minds that spread the decay and further infect our minds. *"A tranquil heart is life to the body, But passion is rottenness to the bones"(Prov 14:30)* Whatever affects our mind will in time affect our bodies. *The Kingdom of*

God is righteousness and peace and joy in the Holy Spirit. (Rom 14: 16-19)

This swarm of flies is likened unto the field within our mind filled with many thoughts, the self-talk where all sin is first birthed. Purity begins in the mind, so whether it's once saved—always saved or sin a little and you're blotted out is insignificant, the point is that our minds need to become transformed, renewed by God and it's only us that can allow that process to take place. It's a choice, moment by moment, thought by thought. If a thought comes to you that is not from God, you are not responsible, however you are responsible if you start to think on it, let it grow and eventually let it influence you in any way. Nip it in the bud! Turn to the Lord and His truth immediately! That might mean excusing yourself to the bathroom to pray, or just refocusing your mind. You know how those commercial jingles get caught in your head and you wind up humming this silly tune all day. That's what you want, however you get to choose the tune. Focus your mind on a worship song, become engulfed in His presence in your heart and the gnat will leave you alone for a time.

Think of King David, every time he would play his harp the tormenting spirits would leave Saul. (1 Sam 16:23; 19:23) Some of us have tormenting spirits assigned to us, but we can put them at bay by worshiping from our hearts; play that music in your heart and the tormenting spirits cannot stay; Light dispels darkness every-time. The enemy cannot stay in the presence of the Lord, worship torments him. Remember Lucifer was the angel of worship until his fall from heaven. It's Satan's greatest pain to hear worship from the hearts of people who are surrendered to the Lord.

Plague #5 Plague against Livestock Ex 9: 1

Our livelihoods, economic stability, provision are all threatened by the limiting, fearful thoughts we have in our lives. It blocks our creativity, and limits our livelihoods. Often this plague is associated with fear and low self-esteem. "What I always feared has happened to me. What I dreaded has come true. I have no peace, no quietness. I have no rest; only trouble comes." (Job 3: 25-26)

When we think that it's us that got us our job or led us into this fabulous career, think again, that's your ego saying "I did it"—realms of soulish thought. God won't share His glory with any one, we would be wise to know that it's God that has blessed us, to focus on our provider and acknowledge that He is in control, not us.

Job lost sight of God, wondered what had happened even despaired of life, he lost everything in this world. Jesus also lost everything, even the presence of the Father on the cross, yet Jesus, for the joy that was set before him endured the cross...He never let go of His focus on His Father's love and purpose for Jesus life here on earth. We too have a purpose, we can be like Job and lose our focus or like Jesus and keep our calling and election sure, obediently following the leading of the Spirit of God to wherever that is, regardless of the cost. For some the cost is their life, yet they joyfully endure because they know it's all a part of God's plan for their lives.

Plague #6 Festering Boils Ex 9:3

Boils cause the flesh to turn dark like a bruise, symbolizes spiritual uncleanness, rejection of salvation. So often our minds get caught up in day to day living and we neglect our spiritual life. We barely open a Bible, pray, read or be a witness. Quickly we start to grow stagnant and as salt we lose our saltiness and are good for nothing spiritually.

The Apostle Paul even had a physical affliction, although theologians disagree as to what it was, I propose that it could have been rooted in a spiritual issue. Our physical lives are only an expression of our inner selves. Everything happens in the spirit first, then soulish realm and finally in our physical bodies. Building and maintaining an intimate relationship with God is Life eternal and it will show in your body, even if God gives the enemy permission to afflict us, our spirits will testify of God's grace through it all.

"So we must listen very carefully to the truth we have heard, or we may drift away from it. For the message God delivered through angels has always stood firm, and every violation of the law and every act of disobedience was punished. So what makes us think we can escape if we ignore this great salvation that was first announced by the Lord Jesus himself and then delivered to us by those who heard him speak? (Heb 2:1-3)

Plague #7 Hail Ex 9:13

Frozen hard water, refers to the hardening of our hearts, stubbornness, rebelliousness, pride. Like thunderous noise in our minds, mental noise and distractions in our self-talk. The many fiery trials we face come directly from our minds, we attract to ourselves fear or faith. It's not a strange thing that these trials come; God places these trials in our lives for our perfecting, it works patience in us and burns off the impurities, all that is not God-like so that we will be refined like pure gold. *"I will hear them: I will say, It is my people: and they will say, 'the Lord is my God'".* (1Pe 4:12,1Pe 1:7, Zec 13:9, Job 23:10 , Jas 1:3)

"But your iniquities have made a separation between you and your God, and your sins have hidden his face from you so that he does not hear" Isa 59:2

"The ones along the path are those who have heard; then the devil comes and takes away the word from their hearts, so that they may not believe and be saved" (Luke 8:12)

"But exhort one another every day, as long as it is called "today," that none of you may be hardened by the deceitfulness of sin" (Heb 3:13)

"But because of your hard and impenitent heart you are storing up wrath for yourself on the day of wrath when God's righteous judgment will be revealed" (Rob 2:5)

"The heart is deceitful above all things, and desperately sick; who can understand it?" (Jer 17:9)

"Keep your heart with all vigilance, for from it flow the springs of life" (Prov 4: 23)

"Trust in the Lord with all your heart, and do not lean on your own understanding" (Prov 3:5)

Plague #8 Locusts Ex 10: 1

Devour the crops. The Word of God is stolen from us. Even from our youth God has placed a vision in your heart, but through the various testing and trials that we face we sometimes lose focus of our visions, sometimes they die. As we renew our first love to the Lord he either renews our vision or gives us a new vision. The locusts have no rights to steal what is rightfully ours unless we through ignorance or wilfully give him permission to steal. Our calling and election are sure, our destiny well mapped out, we simply need to follow the map.

"Consider it pure joy, my brothers and sisters, whenever you face trials of many kinds, because you know that the testing of your faith produces perseverance. Let perseverance finish its work so that you may be mature and

complete, not lacking anything. If any of you lacks wisdom, you should ask God, who gives generously to all without finding fault, and it will be given to you" (James 1:2-5)

We will surrender part to the Lord but not all of our mind. "You must love the LORD your God with all your heart, all your soul, all your strength, and all your mind.' And, 'Love your neighbor as yourself." (Luke 10:27) ""If you love your father or mother more than you love me, you are not worthy of being mine; or if you love your son or daughter more than me, you are not worthy of being mine" (Mtt 10:37)

Plague #9 Darkness Ex 10: 21

Dark night of the Soul

It's a place where you can't see God in your life; a feeling of abandonment from God. Jesus experienced this dark night of the soul. *"Now from the sixth hour darkness fell upon all the land until the ninth hour.And about the ninth hour Jesus cried out with a loud voice, saying,"Eli, Eli, lama sabachthani?" that is, "My God, My God, why hast Thou forsaken Me?" (Mtt 27: 46)*

Many believers go around depressed, disheartened and discouraged during this dark night of the soul, but be encouraged, it's a part of God's plan for His perfecting of His saints. We must go through a little bit of what Jesus went through, we must taste and see that the Lord is good even in the midst of difficult times. It's also an opportunity for the body to surround us and lift our burdens for at this time in our life they are too heavy to carry alone. I always think of sick elephants, when an elephant is not well the other elephants will gather around the sick elephant, so we need the body during times of discouragement. We can carry a backpack (daily trials) but a huge boulder (a major crisis) needs some help from the body of Christ (we are one). Sometimes we don't understand why life must be so painful, physically, emotionally, spiritually. We just need to trust that *"God causes all things to work together for good to those who love God, to those who are called according to His purpose" (Rom 8:28)*

Plague #10 Death of the First born Ex 11: 1

Lastly, Pharoah's plague was the death of the firstborn and with that the children of Israel were set free. The firstborn represents our Adamic nature, the first Adam, our sin/fleshly nature. It's the part of us that wants what we want, our will and base desires. It's that nature that must die before we can enter the promised land of freedom. In North America, and now much of the world we have many people who are living for themselves. A couple of generations ago, the voice of many people would say, "you first"; the next generation said, "me first" and yet there is a further demise in generations with an attitude of "me only". Be careful that you do not fall in the last two categories, but remain in the first who puts God first and then others, rather than seeking your own selfish desires.

"Then he called the crowd to him along with his disciples and said, "If anyone would come after me, he must deny himself and take up his cross and follow me. For whoever wants to save his life will lose it, but whoever loses his life for me and for the gospel will save it." (Mark 8:34-35)

" anyone who does not take his cross and follow me is not worthy of me" (Mat 10:38)

HOMEWORK: Identify each plague usually within your self-talk that has kept you in Egypt until NOW! Write down one statement for each plague that you say in your mind. You do not need to share these thoughts, however it may help someone else in the group if you do.

Plague #1 Blood	
Plague #2 Frogs	
Plague #3 Gnats	
Plague #4 Flies	
Plague #5 Livestock	
Plague #6 Boils	
Plague #7 Hail	
Plague #8 Locusts	
Plague #9 Darkness	
Plague #10 Death of Firstborn	

WEEK #7
OUR VISION, PURPOSE & DESTINY JOURNEY

Our Thoughts determine our Emotions

Our Emotions determine our Actions

Our Actions determine our Habits

Our Habits determine our Character

Our Character determine our Destiny

"Finally, brethren, whatever is true, whatever is honorable, whatever is right, whatever is pure, whatever is lovely, whatever is of good repute, if there is any excellence and if anything worthy of praise, dwell on these things. The things you have learned and received and heard and seen

in me, practice these things, and the God of peace will be with you. (Phil 4:8,9)

Our mind is the seat of our emotions, our goal is to create a seat where our Ego no longer sits but it is inhabited by the presence of God via His Holy Spirit who lives in us. That's a choice, moment by moment that we make to let God sit in that seat, but too often are distracted, rebellious or just plain tired out to pay attention to whom we've allowed in that Holy Place. When that happens, we have all manner of chaos and confusion in our lives. Many of us don't even know who we are, never mind who we are in Christ, or why we're here, our purpose? Didn't even know there was a purpose, oh ya, we're supposed to witness for Jesus...not very personalized, we are all witnesses for Jesus. Our lives are books read by all men. But what about you, can you write your purpose down? Have you? Do you have a mission statement for your life? Did you make it plain? Okay, that's enough! Today is the day to write your life's mission statement, right here, right now; Now is the Time...!

Your purpose in life is to love the Lord your God with all of your hearts and your neighbours as yourself. God's purpose for you is to connect to Him more intimately and more consistently, in doing so you'll connect more to every attribute of the Lord, Love, Joy, Peace, Patience etc. You're fruit will blossom, you'll develop into all that you were intended to be. You'll become Christ-like, manifesting His love, grace and power to those around you. To discover your purpose you'll need to plug in and stay plugged in to God's Spirit. Since your purpose is to intimately connect to God's Spirit in this moment and every moment of your life, then in every choice you'll tap into the voice of the Holy Spirit of God within and do what He would do. Like the old wristband campaign, WWJD. Plug in and Shine for the Lord, express your highest purpose on purpose continually.

EXERCISE: Write your Spiritual Mission Statement.

Knowing God intimately develops the fruit of the Spirit. Knowing God intimately will reveal your purpose. To help you write your mission statement, I have 6 basic questions for you to answer with single word or short phrase answers, afterwards just string these 6 answers together into a meaningful statement--something like this.

"I am a _mother of multitudes_ with a passion to _teach truth_ to _anyone_ who wants to _grow up_ and _discover great hope for their future"_

1. Who you are?

2. What is your passion, what do you love to do?

3. What do you feel qualified to teach others?

4. Who you do it for?

5. What those people want or need?

6. How they changed as a result.?

My Mission Statement:

_____

_____

_____

_____

_____

HOMEWORK: The purpose of your homework is to become more aware of who is sitting on the seat of your mind controlling your emotions. Choose any 24 hour period over the next week, record your behaviour that was troublesome (perhaps a binge), then look at how you were feeling at that time, and what preceded that feeling.

PART #1: Identify one or two emotions that you felt most often over the past few months. What is it?

_____

_____

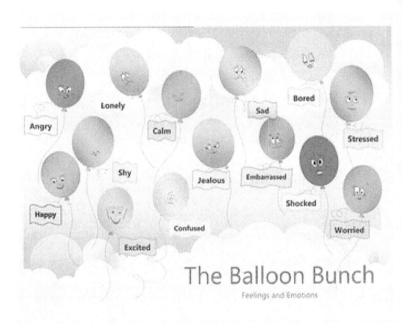

The Balloon Bunch
Feelings and Emotions

Part #2 Keep a record of any troubling behaviours, the emotions and any events preceding or associated with that emotion.

This exercise is used by many therapist to help the client get a better understanding of what they are feeling and what day to day events trigger emotional reactions within them. It's very interesting to learn more about yourself and your triggers for the purpose of disputing your belief about the trigger. It's not the trigger that causes you to behave a certain way, it's your belief about that trigger that results in your behaviour.

Pay attention to what you are feeling and record some of your emotions throughout the day. You'll quickly learn that emotions are fleeting and you'll feel many, many different ones over the course of any 24hr period.

24 HOUR

EMOTIONAL LOG

Time	Troubling Behaviour	How you felt at that time	What happened prior to that
Eg. 6:30	Binge on cookies	Tired, upset	Received a bill in the mail for $400. I thought I'd paid it already.

You may use another sheet of paper for the Emotional Log if you feel it's necessary.

After recording your emotions look at your beliefs about yourself at that time; see if there is a theme behind your believes, then dispute those beliefs so that next time this or a similar event happens you can do something more beneficial rather than your dysfunctional patterns of behaviour.

For example, you may have believed that you are weak or inadequate in some way. However, God says that *"For the sake of Christ, then, I am content with weaknesses, insults, hardships, persecutions, and calamities. For when I am weak, then I am strong" (2 Cor 12:10)*

Record here One scripture that disputes the theme that arose in your emotional log.

_____

_____

_____

_____

_____

_____

WEEK #8

LAW & ORDER

Diet rules (law) = Bondage

Spirit led (order) = Freedom in Christ

We're taking back self-control with blossoming fruit

"Therefore there is now no condemnation for those who are in Christ Jesus. For the law of the Spirit of life in Christ Jesus has set you free from the law of sin and of death. For what the Law could not do, weak as it was through the flesh, God did: sending His own Son in the likeness of sinful flesh and as an offering for sin, He condemned sin in the flesh– Christ came to set us free from the law of sin & death" (Rom 8:1-3)

The law by definition is a prescribed set of rules and regulations to regulate the actions of the members of a society, enforced by penalties for disobedience. According to the Talmud (written traditions of Jewish elders) there are

95

613 mitzvot ("commandments") in the Torah. As a Kingdom citizen *"sin is no longer your master, for you no longer live under the requirements of the law. Instead, you live under the freedom of God's grace" (Rom 6:14)* Today, we hear a lot of talk about the new world order. The new world order is nothing more than an old order resurrecting. It's an extreme measure of control and domination; that is not what God has for His people; those who love, trust and obey Him. God has an order that He is establishing along-side the kingdoms of this world; like the wheat and the tares they grow up at the same time.

The Kingdom of Heaven has a divine order. God chose to work through an individual, whom He sent to earth as a man, His only son Jesus Christ. This person (which is how Jesus walked while on this earth) said, *"I am the way, the truth, and the life: no man comes to the Father, but by Me" (John 14:6)*. Jesus gave His Holy Spirit to the church as a comforter and teacher who would lead every believer into all truth; the Holy Spirit gave gifts to every believer (Acts 2:38). None of these are earned by ourselves, they are gifts. Each of us has different gifts but all for the same purpose of edifying, strengthening, feeding, exhorting, encouraging, witnessing, basically building up the Body of Christ.

Within the body he's placed order.

Five-fold Governmental Gifts: Apostles who are founders and touch all of the 5 – fold governmental ministries in the Church. Prophets who point the way, see ahead and share the mind of the Lord on matters. Both Apostle and Prophets are foundational to the Church; Evangelists have a passion for the lost; Pastors care for and shepherd the people of their flock; Teachers, share what God is saying with a very high level accountability for rightly dividing the Word of Truth. All five of these governmental gifts were given.

9 Gifts of Holy Spirit: Word of Knowledge; Word of Wisdom; Gift of Prophecy; Gift of Faith; Gifts of Healings; Working of Miracles: Discerning of Spirits; Different Kinds of Tongues; Interpretation of Tongues.

9 Fruit of the Spirit: (Gal 5:22-23) Love; Joy; Peace; Longsuffering; Kindness; Goodness; Faithfulness; Gentleness; Self-Control

There are many more gifts, just as important and valuable to the Body of Christ, yet often times not as visible. *"For even as the body is one and yet has many members, and all the members of the body, though they are many, are one body, so also is Christ" (1 Cor 12:12)* Gifts of helps and administration just to name a few, every part of the body is important, just as *"the eye cannot say to the hand, "I have no need of you"; or again the head to the feet, "I have no need of you" (1 Cor 12:21)* we cannot say that we don't need some part of the body. We need all of us fully functioning in spirit, soul and body and that's why these teachings exist that we would all grow up into our rightful place in the body.

The days of putting individuals on pedestals and worshiping man are over. We did a dis-service to the Church, to those in positions of leadership and to the Christ Himself by worshiping man. I honor the place of leadership with those who I submit to but I do not worship them, they are only men on the same mission side by side with me and you. Each of us has a necessary part in the body of Christ, regardless of the part, whether an eye, ear or part of the spiritual inner nervous system, we need optimal functioning free from bondage of any kind, except being a bond-servant of Jesus Christ.

As bond-servants of Jesus Christ we are free from the bondage to human rules of behaviour; *"Therefore do not*

97

let anyone judge you by what you eat or drink, or with regard to a religious festival, a New Moon celebration or a Sabbath day. These are a shadow of the things that were to come; the reality, however, is found in Christ. Do not let anyone who delights in false humility and the worship of angels disqualify you. Such a person also goes into great detail about what they have seen; they are puffed up with idle notions by their unspiritual mind. They have lost connection with the head, from whom the whole body, supported and held together by its ligaments and sinews, grows as God causes it to grow.

Since you died with Christ to the elemental spiritual forces of this world, why, as though you still belonged to the world, do you submit to its rules: "Do not handle! Do not taste! Do not touch!"? These rules, which have to do with things that are all destined to perish with use, are based on merely human commands and teachings. Such regulations indeed have an appearance of wisdom, with their self-imposed worship, their false humility and their harsh treatment of the body, but they lack any value in restraining sensual indulgence" (Col 2:16-23)

TAKING BACK SELF CONTROL: *Blossoming Fruit – Trusting & Obeying the Holy Spirit's leading and taking our rightful place in the body of Christ.*

A man without self-control is like a city broken into and left without walls. (Prov 25:28)

No temptation has overtaken you that is not common to man. God is faithful, and he will not let you be tempted beyond your ability, but with the temptation he will also provide the way of escape, that you may be able to endure it. (1 Cor 10:33)

But the fruit of the Spirit is love, joy, peace, patience, kindness, goodness, faithfulness, gentleness, self-control; against such things there is no law. (Gal 5:22-23)

We're like grapes on God's vine, initially a grape is only a dormant bud, also called an "eye" is actually compound with 3 growing points within the one bud. The dormant bud is the focal point during dormant pruning, since it contains the cluster primordia (the fruit producing potential for the next season). The dormant bud undergoes considerable development in the season prior to growing fruit. The three growing points bud, each producing a shoot which later develop into a fully grown shoot with leaves, tendrils, and in some cases flower clusters. The flower cluster represents the fruiting potential of the bud in the following season. Dormant buds that develop under unfavorable conditions (shade of a dense canopy, poor nutrition, etc) produce fewer flower clusters and therefore less fruit. As in our lives, we are like the dormant bud, the eye; during pruning we are the part that is pruned so that we can bring forth more fruit, however if the conditions that we live in are dark, or have poor nutrition, there are few flower clusters therefore less fruit for that season. In our lives the cares of this world; an overshadowing fear over us, and a lack of good spiritual nutrition can cause a fruit shortage in our lives. Season after season of fruit shortage in the area of self-control may be the reason why you're here today. Notice that it's 'fruit of the Spirit' not 'fruits' although some modern versions pluralize the verb (not noun), it's really singular because it's God's fruit, not part of a grape but the whole deal. He does not show favoritism, we have all the fruit of the Spirit dormant with within us, it's just a matter of changing the canopy over us and eating proper nutrition to bring out the best harvest of fruit for our Master--His Banner of Love over us and our feasting at His table is His desire for us. We've been called to be fruit bearers for the Kingdom, to do so we must become like the King.

Your purpose in life is to love the Lord your God with all of your hearts and your neighbours as yourself. God's purpose for you is to connect to Him more intimately and more consistently, in doing so you'll connect more to every attribute of the Lord, Love, Joy, Peace, Patience etc. You'll become Christ-like, manifesting His love, grace and power to those around you. To discover your purpose you'll need to plug in and stay plugged in to God's Spirit. Since your purpose is to intimately connect to God's spirit in this moment and every moment of your life, then in every choice you'll tap into the voice of the Holy Spirit of God within and do what He would do. Like the old wristband campaign, WWJD. Plug in and Shine for the Lord, express your highest purpose on purpose continually.

HOMEWORK: Write your Spiritual Mission Statement.

Knowing God intimately develops the fruit of the Spirit. Knowing God intimately will reveal your purpose. To help you write your mission statement, I have 6 basic questions for you to answer with single word or short phrase answers, then just string these 6 answers together into a meaningful statement--something like this.

"I am a mother of multitudes with a passion to teach Truth to anyone who wants to grow up and discover great hope for their future"

7. Who you are?
8. What is your passion, what do you love to do?
9. What do you feel qualified to teach others?
10. Who you do it for?
11. What those people need?
12. How will they be changed as a result?

My   Mission   Statement:_____
_____
_____
_____

Happy people like to make others happy and they receive the happiness back.

For this very reason, make every effort to supplement your faith with virtue, and virtue with knowledge, and knowledge with self-control, and self-control with steadfastness, and steadfastness with godliness, and godliness with brotherly affection, and brotherly affection with love. (2 Pet 1:5-7)

Do you not know that in a race all the runners run, but only one receives the prize? So run that you may obtain it. Every athlete exercises self-control in all things. They do it to receive a perishable wreath, but we an imperishable. So I do not run aimlessly; I do not box as one beating the air. But I discipline my body and keep it under control, lest after preaching to others I myself should be disqualified. (1 Cor 9:24-27)

But I discipline my body and keep it under control, lest after preaching to others I myself should be disqualified. (1 Cor 9:27)

Whoever is slow to anger is better than the mighty, and he who rules his spirit than he who takes a city. (Prov 16:32)

For God gave us a spirit not of fear but of power and love and self-control. (2 Tim 1:7)

The end of all things is at hand; therefore be self-controlled and sober-minded for the sake of your prayers. (1 Pet 4:7)

"For the grace of God has appeared, bringing salvation for all people, training us to renounce ungodliness and worldly passions, and to live self-controlled, upright, and godly lives in the present age, waiting for our blessed hope, the appearing of the glory of our great God and Savior Jesus Christ, who gave himself for us to redeem us from all lawlessness and to purify for himself a people for his own possession who are zealous for good works" (Titus 2:11-14)

"But hospitable, a lover of good, self-controlled, upright, holy, and disciplined" (Titus 1:8)

"Training us to renounce ungodliness and worldly passions, and to live self-controlled, upright, and godly lives in the present age", (Titus 2:12)

"I appeal to you therefore, brothers, by the mercies of God, to present your bodies as a living sacrifice, holy and acceptable to God, which is your spiritual worship. Do not be conformed to this world, but be transformed by the renewal of your mind, that by testing you may discern what is the will of God, what is good and acceptable and perfect" (Rom 12:1-2)

"Finally, brothers, whatever is true, whatever is honorable, whatever is just, whatever is pure, whatever is lovely, whatever is commendable, if there is any excellence, if there is anything worthy of praise, think about these things". (Phil 4:8)

"Every athlete exercises self-control in all things. They do it to receive a perishable wreath, but we an imperishable" (1 Cor 9:25)

"For we do not wrestle against flesh and blood, but against the rulers, against the authorities, against the cosmic

powers over this present darkness, against the spiritual forces of evil in the heavenly places". (Eph 6:12)

"Or do you not know that your body is a temple of the Holy Spirit within you, whom you have from God, and that you are not your own? For you have been bought with a price: therefore glorify God in your body" (1 Cor 6:19-20)

"Do you not know that in a race all the runners run, but only one receives the prize? So run that you may obtain it. Every athlete exercises self-control in all things. They do it to receive a perishable wreath, but we an imperishable". (1 Cor 9:24-25)

"I can do all things through him who strengthens me" (Phil 4:13)

"And Jesus, full of the Holy Spirit, returned from the Jordan and was led by the Spirit in the wilderness for forty days, being tempted by the devil. And he ate nothing during those days. And when they were ended, he was hungry. The devil said to him, "If you are the Son of God, command this stone to become bread." And Jesus answered him, "It is written, 'Man shall not live by bread alone.'" And the devil took him up and showed him all the kingdoms of the world in a moment of time" (Luke 4:1-44)

"But I say, walk by the Spirit, and you will not gratify the desires of the flesh. For the desires of the flesh are against the Spirit, and the desires of the Spirit are against the flesh, for these are opposed to each other, to keep you from doing the things you want to do" (Gal 5: 16-17)

"I appeal to you therefore, brothers, by the mercies of God, to present your bodies as a living sacrifice, holy and acceptable to God, which is your spiritual worship" (Rom 12:1)

"For those who live according to the flesh set their minds on the things of the flesh, but those who live according to the Spirit set their minds on the things of the Spirit. For to set the mind on the flesh is death, but to set the mind on the Spirit is life and peace" (Rom 8:5-6)

"For the weapons of our warfare are not of the flesh but have divine power to destroy strongholds. We destroy arguments and every lofty opinion raised against the knowledge of God, and take every thought captive to obey Christ" (2 Cor 10:4-5)

"All things are lawful for me," but not all things are helpful. "All things are lawful for me," but I will not be enslaved by anything" (1 Cor 6:12)

"For if you live according to the flesh you will die, but if by the Spirit you put to death the deeds of the body, you will live" (Rom 8:13)

"Let not sin therefore reign in your mortal body, to make you obey its passions" (Rom 6:12)

WEEK #9

LOVE

– covers a multitude of sins

ALTRUISM (highest God nature in us, LOVE)

vs EGO (our lowest sin nature)

Altruism is the highest expression of love. It's the man who runs into a burning building to sleeping teenager, or the stranger giving a kidney to someone they've barely met; the highest expression of Love was God's gift of His son as the perfect Lamb of God who died on the cross taking upon himself the punishment for the sins that we have done. Thank-you Jesus, we didn't deserve it, yet you've saved all of us who believe upon you. Those who love you obey you. Help us Lord to become obedient in all things without hesitation or reservation.

For every habit that we have or experience that we repeatedly go through, every pattern that's repeated in our lives, there is a need within us for it to happen. That need corresponds to some belief that we have about ourselves. If we did not have a perceived need, then we wouldn't have to do it. There is something within us that needs more food, bad choices of food, or poor relationships, co-dependencies, failures, cigarettes, crack, cutting, alcohol, gambling, anger, poverty, abuse or whatever the problem is for us. It's not a matter of willpower alone. It's a matter of a deep need within us that we need to release to the Lord. The key factor is, are we willing to release the need to the Lord and let go of our striving to control? Be patient as you unravel the mysterious ball of twine that's developed to hold those thoughts neatly nestled within your soul. Willingness to let go is the first step, and continuing to love yourself throughout the transformation process as you re-align your thought processes to God's Word spoken to your heart. Jesus is always fighting on your behalf to succeed, if you continue to look to Him and follow the principles of The Kingdom Weigh, you will have Victory over sin/self/Satan in your life.

If I were to give you a diet to follow, you would not be set free, you would become enslaved to another man-made law. Every outer effect is the natural expression of an inner thought pattern. To battle only the outer effect or symptom is wasted energy and often increases the problem. Most people who diet, do so repeatedly until dieting itself becomes the strong-hold. Let's break that, eating the Kingdom Weigh! (way)

Love is the answer to all things. Years ago an adoption TV show's theme song was, "All you need is love". On so many levels that is true, since God is Love, He displays His love all around us, in us to the world through us. Certainly, when God brings chastisement into the lives of those He loves it is as painful, if not more than a physical rod of correction. The 'rod of God'' separates the waters so we can pass through to the promised land, it's a scepter of authority, a symbol of the King's power, and instrument of miracles, it disciplines, drives out the foolishness bound up in the spiritual child, it brings reproof and gives wisdom all for our good so that we can become mature in Christ. (Ex 21:20; Ex 4:20; 7:9, 12:19; Prov 3:11-12; Heb 12: 5-11; Prov 22:15; Prov 29:15)

When I look at my earlier motivators, I was motivated to "get back on track" out of anger; angry that I did this to my body (again). One of my major discoveries is that I was wrong, again. Anger was not the way to be successful or become healthy.

Emotions have a huge effect on the internal workings of our body. Some people try to departmentalize thoughts, emotions and weight loss but that is impossible because each one affects the other, either through anger or love. Your emotions have an effect on your whole way of existing. Your thoughts and emotions determine every behavior ranging from interpersonal skills, self-destructive behaviors, even the neurochemicals and molecular structure of your body. This revelation was life changing for me.

Anger is a motivator that negatively affects our body in the same way, negatively. Just think of how you feel when someone that you care about is angry with you, how saddened you are, perhaps even sending you into a tailspin of despair or depression or causing you to become aggressive with others. Basically, it can set you up for a bad day.

Love on the other hand also affects your body, only this time in a very positive sense. Now think about when someone you care about expresses love to you, a nice comment, gesture or affection in some way. You feel good, don't you? Not only do you feel good, but since our thoughts determine our emotions, and our emotions determine behavior, those thoughts empower or disempower you and all of it began with your thoughts. Were they based in Anger, or in Love? It's true in therapy that you could affect change by focusing on your behavior, or on the emotion but if you want long lasting, lifestyle change the focus has to be in the mind. Renewing your mind, setting your thoughts on things that are good, loving and kind towards yourself, that's a part of loving yourself and if you love yourself, you'll treat yourself through that love by caring for yourself.

Now, the question is, "do you care about you?" If you do, then from this day forward it's a time to love yourself. Not egotistical, or self-absorbed, but genuine love. Yes, you may overeat, or all out binge from time to time, either because you're hurting, celebrating, or whatever the emotional trigger is, you overeat. You could have paid attention to your emotions and thoughts before the binge, but you didn't. Your behavior gets out of hand, you seem to lose control of yourself. It can happen, but if it does, you have the power to determine your reaction to the behavior, you can be angry with yourself, or you can love yourself, love your health, your fitness, just love feeling good.

There are more neurochemicals released from the digestive tract than from the brain. Neurochemicals are released every time we feel an emotion, the accumulative effect of those neurochemicals leads to either health or sickness in body, soul and spirit. Choose this day to change it, change your thoughts, change your emotions and your behavior will change. Guaranteed! That's why the Lord says to renew your mind daily by relationship with God for He is LOVE. LOVE is the Master Key to holistic wellness.

Change the way that you think about yourself, love yourself. Allow yourself to feel the host of emotions that come with that love; name every good thing about you and as you do your thoughts will lead to positive caring behaviors.

You are so loved that the God of the Universe(s) sent His very own son to take the penalty for all of your sins. That is the ultimate expression of love, surely we can express a measure of that love towards ourselves.

So this is what happens when we feel...

ANGER	LOVE
Cells become agitated	Fluids between cells change, causing cells to cling together
You feel sad, weak or worthless	Energized
Lack energy	Psychologically strong
Psychologically irrational, distorted thoughts	Release of serotonin, makes you feel good
Release of adrenaline and noradrenaline that hinders weight loss	Strong intra and inter relationships
Ready to fight yourself or flight (give up)	Kindness exudes from you
Hindered intra and inter relationships	Victory
Abusive, rude tendencies	Ownership of yourself
Self-pity	
Blaming others	
Suppressed immune system, HBP, IBS, and other physiological problems	

Unfortunately, far too many of us have a twisted view of God as an old man beating his children into submission with a stick (the rod of correction). Without getting into the debates over corporal punishment, the rod basically represents authority, in this case the King's authority. Since we know that God is Love we don't need to fear His reproof, His correction, His chastening in our lives because He only chastens those whom He loves. Count it all joy as Jesus did, even to the point of the cross. There is nothing that comes into your life that God does not see and allow for a divine purpose to be worked in or through you. Love says "all things work together for good to those who love God and are called according to His purpose" (Rom 8:28) If we love God back, we will do what He says continually

(John 14: 15) If you don't do what God says, you are a liar and the truth is not in you (1 John 2:4) But those who obey whatever He speaks to you truly shows how completely they love Him. That is how we know that we are living in Him. (1 John 2:5) *We have come to know and have believed the love which God has for us. God is love, and the one who abides in love abides in God, and God abides in him. By this, love is perfected with us, so that we may have confidence in the day of judgment; because as He is, so also are we in this world. There is no fear in love; but perfect love casts out fear, because fear involves punishment, and the one who fears is not perfected in love....(1 John 4:17)*

"Love is patient, love is kind and is not jealous; love does not brag and is not arrogant, does not act unbecomingly; it does not seek its own, is not provoked, does not take into account a wrong suffered, does not rejoice in unrighteousness, but rejoices with the truth; bears all things, believes all things, hopes all things, endures all things.

Love never fails; but if there are gifts of prophecy, they will be done away; if there are tongues, they will cease; if there is knowledge, it will be done away. For we know in part and we prophesy in part; but when the perfect comes, the partial will be done away. When I was a child, I used to speak like a child, think like a child, reason like a child; when I became a man, I did away with childish things. For now we see in a mirror dimly, but then face to face; now I know in part, but then I will know fully just as I also have been fully known. But now faith, hope, love, abide these three; but the greatest of these is love" (1 Cor 13: 4-13)

When we read the famous love chapter, read at most weddings and many funerals we usually project that love outward, which is good, however, sometimes we fail to reflect that love inwards. In other words we speak kindness and do acts of kindness and love to most everyone we meet. We give them all that we have and more, but we fail to treat ourselves with the same love and kindness that we show to others. When God says to love our neighbours as ourselves, we do that well. Perhaps your parents loved you with all that they had to love, but they were deficient in some way. We do may deficient in some way, the love in us is not made complete. When we do something unwise like going through a stop sign when driving, we quickly retort, "stupid idiot" to the driver of our vehicle—ourselves. When we eat a huge bowl of icecream though we weren't hungry, we say in our hearts, "what a pig"; or we look in the mirror when no one is around and see a totally different picture than those models in their skimpy swimwear, we say, "fat slob". Then to top it off we get angry with ourselves and decide to punish ourselves in some harsh way, because we deserve to be punished in our minds. So we design the torment to make us suffer more, we will punish ourselves starting tomorrow by going on a very strict diet, a new set of laws that we lay down for ourselves, or download off the Internet: we will never eat bread, icecream or whatever perceived evil food that think we need to be punished with.

This is NOT love, it does not come from the place of love and is not how you should be treating a Child of the Most High God. Love within is calling you to manifest His love to yourself. *"The power of Love within us has given us everything that we need to live a life of godliness (god-like-ness), through the true knowledge of Him who has called us to His own glory and excellence. For by these He has granted to us His precious and magnificent promises, so that by them you may become partakers of the divine nature, having escaped the corruption that is in the world by lust...."* (2 Peter 1:3)

What would happen if the next time we eat something un-healthy, or a little too much of your favourite treat, or perhaps we didn't exercise much for a while, perhaps not at all. Rather than beating ourselves up for it, we bring ourselves to repentance through kindness, just as God does? "..do you suppose this, O man, when you pass judgment on those who practice such things and do the same yourself, that you will escape the judgment of God? Or do you think lightly of the riches of His kindness and tolerance and patience, not knowing that the kindness of God leads you to repentance? But because of your stubbornness and unrepentant heart you are storing up wrath for yourself in the day of wrath and revelation of the righteous judgment of God,..." (Rom 2:4)

What if we started to love ourselves unconditionally, like God does? What would happen if would no longer pass judgment on us but would practice forgiveness, kindness, tolerance and patience, not jealous because someone else has the body we want, nor boastful because we lost weight, we did nothing except for the grace and love of God in us did we lose weight (never take the glory, it belongs to God), no more being rude to ourselves, what if we didn't demand that we diet or live by man-made rules? Or secretly rejoice because our increase on the scales proves to us that we are genetically flawed for excess or this is just how God wants me to be. NO, let it not be so with you my sister or brother! Love never gives up, love never loses faith, is always hopeful and endures through every circumstance.

Practice Time! Let's start practicing, the more you practice at anything the better you'll become. Let's start practicing loving ourselves with God's love from within so that we can live a life that is an epistle of God read of all men. The people around us will see God in and through us, we won't have to learn the Roman road to salvation, how to witness in 30 seconds or any other formula. We will be a witness to the lost, we will be a voice of truth, we will be Love manifested on the earth. We will please our Lord and walk in His ways, becoming conformed to His image more and more each day.

Are you with me?

"Choose for yourselves this day whom you will serve" (Joshua 24:15). "...speaking the truth in love, we are to grow up in every way into him who is the head, into Christ" (Eph 4:15). "Confess your sins one to another, pray for one another that you will be healed, the prayer of a righteous person is powerful and effective" (James 5:16). "Intercede for each other...until Christ is formed in you!" (Gal 4:19)

Love God, treat yourself with God's Love. *It's His kindness, forbearance and patience that leads us to repentance (Rom 2:4).* not His punishment or cruelty but joy in the Holy Spirit. These things will last eternally, *Faith, hope, love but the greatest of these is Love (1 Cor 13:13)*

Love is a place that is higher than this earthly realm, a place to aspire to in all of its fullness a Utopia with no fear only perfect love, perfect peace and rest for our souls.

HOMEWORK Part #1: Look daily in your eyes in the mirror, focus deep in your eyes, the window of your soul, as you speak, *"I love you...**your name**...I've called you by name for such a time as this that you will be my...**hands/voice/feet.** here on earth. Please care for my holy temple while you live in it; for you need it to accomplish my best through your life"* It's an exercise of Christ in you speaking to you. Although the Bible does not specifically say that our eyes are the window of our soul, it

113

implies that if our eye is full of light (truth) then our entire being will be full of truth and will align with the truth. *"Your eye is a lamp that provides light for your body. When your eye is good, your whole body is filled with light"* Mtt 6:22.

HOMEWORK, Part #2: Write down your feelings as you spoke into the reflection in the mirror.

As I spoke *"I love you...**your name**...I've called you by name for such a time as this that you will be my...**hands/voice/feet**..here on earth. Please care for my holy temple while you live in it; for you need it to accomplish my best through your life"* I felt:

_____

_____

_____

_____

_____

_____

_____

WEEK #10

BUMPS, ROADBLOCKS, STUMBLING AND PRIDE

I've lived in Canada for most of my life. The winters are brutal to our roads, the freezing and defrosting cause the roads asphalt to break up so that we have major pot holes that continually keep our road crews busy. Thanks guys for fixing our roads! I've had times where I've driven and suddenly I hit a major bump in the road, even broke an axle once on a new car. Usually there is a sign that says "bump ahead" giving warning that you must slow down to go over the bump. During road and bridge repairs there are often detours so they'll put a road block up and we'll have to go a different way.

Our walk with God in this world is kind of like that. Although we are in this world we are not a part of this world, we are driving along in His vehicle, our bodies AND we hit a bump in the road. It could be work, family pressures, relationship problems, illness, the cares of this world can all cause bumps in our roads. It doesn't feel good, you don't like it, sometimes it's the deepest hurt and pains imaginable and you wonder where God went. Remember that nothing can happen to you without God's permission. Like Job, Satan has to get permission to touch you from God or else He can't touch you. *""But put forth Your hand now and touch all that he has; he will surely curse You to Your face." Then the LORD said to Satan,*

"Behold, all that he has is in your power, only do not put forth your hand on him." So Satan departed from the presence of the LORD" (Job 1:12) If there is stress of any kind and we allow it to fester, then it can cause psychological problems, depression, anxiety and a host of other mental health problems, and/or it can show up in our bodies, aches, pains, even debilitating diseases.

Sometimes it's necessary to take a detour because there is a blockage. This is much like the process of breaking a bad habit or addiction. Our brains need to learn or relearn a new pattern by making new neuro-connections; new patterns of thought which will manifest in new patterns of action.

The word "addiction" is derived from a Latin term for "enslaved by" or "bound to." Anyone who has struggled to overcome an addiction—or has tried to help someone else to do so—understands why.

Addictions have a very powerful influence on the brain that expresses itself in three distinct ways: craving for the object of addiction, loss of control over its use, and continuing involvement with it despite adverse consequences.

By definition that would include many of you as having an addiction. When I first started to study addictions for a course that I was designing to teach in College, I carefully studied the research and was shocked to discover that I had an addiction, 100% addiction to caffeine. I thought I just liked coffee, but no, it was more than that. I consumed a good 2 pots, maybe 3 per day. I stopped caffeine that day. Since then, it's a rare day that I have caffeine, usually only when out with others, but it no longer has a hold on me. Many addictions are clear cut, in that you can stop them and live a full life. Our bodies don't need crack cocaine, gambling, alcohol, cigarettes…but food? Well we do need food, but we don't need an addiction to food. So this area is a little more grey, which gives us the opportunity to make excuses. Fortunately we've already dealt with Excuses in Week #1, so we won't pick up any more excuses.

Eating is all about balance, taking in the amount and best nutritional choices available, while focusing on the Giver of the food, the giver of every good and perfect gift. Food is a good thing; money is a good thing, if used properly. If not, when misused or abused through greed, lack of restraint it can bring destruction to many areas of our lives. We've been saved from a life of bondage and given a life of freedom and abundant vitality. Jesus says *"I am the door; if anyone enters through Me, he will be saved, and will go in and out and find pasture. "The thief comes only to steal and kill and destroy; I came that they may have life, and have it abundantly. "I am the good shepherd; the good shepherd lays down His life for the sheep. ...*(Jn 10: 9-11)

When we surrender to the enemy of our soul's prompting for over-indulgence in anything we surrender God's best for the strongholds of the enemy to begin to develop. We open the door to sin through our own lusts. Then the LORD said to Cain, *"Why are you angry? And why has your countenance fallen? "If you do well, will not your countenance be lifted up? And if you do not do well, sin is crouching at the door; and its desire is for you, but you must master it." (Gen 4:7)*

For many years, experts believed that only alcohol and powerful drugs could cause addiction. Neuroimaging technologies and more recent research, however, have shown that certain pleasurable activities, such as gambling, shopping, and sex, even food can apprehend our brains and bring it into bondage. They all start with pleasure and end in compulsion, so the 'victim' does what they don't want to do and the good that they do want to do they don't do.

None of those things are inherently wrong, but misused they can lead to slavery to sin. They all involve pleasure seeking and the various hormones that are released in pleasure, Dopamine, Adreneline, Catecholamines, Endorphines, Seratonin and a number of other neurotransmitters depending on the actions of the substance of the addiction. The various paths also play a significant role, for our purposes we're discussing ingested substances. Did you know sugar is a drug, caffeine is a poison? Maybe these things ought not to used so liberally in the temple of the Holy Spirit, just thinking ;) If it looks sounds too good, looks too good, taste too good...beware! That's what they say when you're looking for scammers in advertising, perhaps that's exactly what the enemy is doing, he's advertising his (fake) goodness to those who are weak, vulnerable.

Never let your guard down! The way to do that is not to be watching for little demons scurrying around in your living-room but to be drawing closer and closer to the Great I AM who lives within you through the person of the Holy Spirit. Get to know Him, listen to Him and know that He has great plans for you, for your life. They are plans for good and not for evil, to prosper and give you hope. (Jer 29:11) Love (God) is everything that you need. Even if the nutrition that you have is less than optimal, stay connected closely to Him, ask Him and He will bless it because He's Love manifested. Even if it's poison, and there is nothing else but you're forced to consume it, it will not harm you. Don't get so caught up in your thoughts, discussions, and time with what to eat, get a new hunger for spiritual food, for God, His goodness, His exciting life and the rest will just follow...you will know abundant life. Focus on Love (God) in every breath you take, every moment your awake, or asleep, He's speaking we just need to tune in. Get the focus off of changing others and start changing yourself from deep within. God is pleased with our hearts of obedience and His greatest desire is to co-labour with you, in the purpose that he has for you.

There may be bumps in your road, there may be roadblocks where you need to take a new path, or you may fall, but the root of all sin boils down to pride. Humble yourself before the Lord, walk in humility and continue to examine your own heart before Him and He will keep you from pride, stumbling and falling.

Today, as in the day of Isaiah there is a voice of one crying in the wilderness, in the barren places of our egos, 'Make ready the way of the Lord, Make His paths straight.' Every ravine will be filled, and every mountain and hill will be brought low: the crooked will become straight, and the rough roads smooth; and all flesh will see the salvation of God"

So it will be that when… you return to the Lord your God and obey Him with all your heart and soul according to all that I command you today, you and your sons, then the Lord your God will restore you from captivity *(all manner of bondages, addictions, spirits of anger, jealousy etc)*, and have *compassion* on you. If…then… The Lord your God will bring you into the land which your fathers possessed, and you shall possess it; and He will prosper you and multiply you more than your fathers (Deut 30:2-5)

Moreover the Lord your God will circumcise your heart and the heart of your descendants, to love the Lord your God with all your heart and with all your soul, so that you may live.

God's promises are yes and Amen, but you must read the "If statements" If we do….then God promises. It's an age old parenting technique, "when/then" I said that many times to my own children. When you've finished cleaning your room, we'll go to the park. God says the same, "if (when) you decide to love me with your whole heart, soul, mind and strength, then I will deliver you from your bondages"

I don't know about you, but that looks pretty straightforward to me, and it sounds like a very good deal, I'm totally in! How about you?

"Temptation comes from our own desires, which entice us and drag us away. These desires give birth to sinful actions. And when sin is allowed to grow, it gives birth to death" (James 1: 14-15)

"Pride comes before destruction, and an arrogant spirit before a fall" Prov 16:18

"Humble yourselves before the Lord, and he will lift you up," it says in James 4:10. We hear the same idea echoed in the Gospel: "For whoever exalts himself will be humbled, and whoever humbles himself will be exalted" (Matthew 23:12). God honours us when we are humble, in part because we are open to His guidance. It's only then that He can show us what is right and teach us in His way (Psalm 25:9).

-"God opposes the proud but gives grace to the humble" (1 Peter 5:5)

" Those who exalt themselves will be humbled, and those who humble themselves will be exalted" (Luke 14:11)

"But take care that this liberty of yours does not somehow become a stumbling block to the weak" (1 Cor 8:9)

Perhaps you are that weak one, perhaps eating around certain people causes you to stumble, or putting yourself in tempting situations, like Mandarin Buffet. If that causes you, or someone else to stumble then stay away. Remove temptation from yourself and others, clean out your home, if you can, of those things that tempt you. Initially, that was all baked goods for me, perhaps for you it's something else.

We are free to eat all things in moderation, as we follow the Spirit of God within us, He will lead us into the foods that we need, the portion sizes and the frequency. It's that simple!

Surrender of self, forgiveness of others, examining self before the Lord and praising Him for truly it is only the Lord that can make us into His image. We simply need to let go of ourselves so that He can have control of all of us.

Psalty the Singing Song Book, Kid's Song: Take all of me, take all of me, to a world that's lost help me count the cost take all of me. *"Whoever does not carry his own cross and come after Me cannot be My disciple. "For which one of you, when he wants to build a tower, does not first sit down and calculate the cost to see if he has enough to complete it?" (Luke 14:27-28)*

HOMEWORK: in every time of temptation, look for God's way of escape and record what happened

"No temptation has overtaken you that is not common to man. God is faithful, and he will not let you be tempted beyond your ability, but with the temptation he will also provide the way of escape, that you may be able to endure it" (1 Cor 10:13)

Temptation	God's way of Escape
Eg. Chocolate cake with creamy icing	Just as I was about to endulge my flesh, my son

121

	popped down the stairs and said, "is that for me". Immediately, I said, "yes" and thanked the Lord that this slim, energetic teenager was sent by the Lord as my way of escape
Temptation:	Escape:
Temptation:	Escape:
Temptation:	Escape:
Temptation:	Escape:
Temptation:	Escape:

WEEK #11

CO-CREATORS OF OUR DESTINY

We will become what we hunger for—Hunger for Righteousness!

God gives us the desires of our heart (those Godly) desires were placed there by God Himself)

God is a creator, He lives within us. The kingdom of Heaven is within, therefore we, through the Spirit of God within have the power to create. If that is so, then why do we see such a lack of power in the church? Good question, let's start with ourselves to answer it. Jesus says, *"I and the Father are one" (Jn 10:30).* Good point, in fact, that is the point. If we are in perfect alignment with the purposes of God, totally surrendered to God's will in every breath, every thought, every movement of our days we'll begin to bring forth the manifestations that He desires of us. To do that we need to die to our will, crucify our flesh nature, our ego, and live in Christ. The great "I AM" is resident within you. As you ponder that for just a moment, His presence is overwhelming, that He would choose to take up residence in this temple is beyond comprehension, yet it's 100% true, it's the reality that God desires we begin to walk in. When I think of the Great I AM, and how He has made me in His image, I need to look into His image to see what it is that I am. A brief English lesson: First of all God is not a noun, God is a verb. He says "I AM" which describes a state of being. God is all about action, He never slumbers or sleeps, He creates, He loves, comforts, provides, cares for me, leads, orders, heals, saves and finally sanctifies me. He is the one today who is working within each one of us to bring us into the one-ness with the I AM. I am His; I am in The I AM and the I AM is in me. That in itself is amazing!

I am growing in the grace, power and love of the I AM that I would manifest His desires here on earth in the place(s) with the people that He desires, in the way that He desires. His will is mine. May your Kingdom come and your will be done on earth...*through this earthen vessel*...as it is in Heaven.

The names of the Great I AM, JEHOVAH, God are all about His Actions. God is verb, God is LOVE! As you read each one of the 12 names (actions) of God just think of how He manifests each one of these in your life and how you can manifest Him in other people's lives. Can you be a strength for another, protect another, heal another, be there for them, provide for them, bring peace. If God is the Great I AM then I propose that I am able to do the same within His leading and within His plans and purposes.

In fact, Jesus said, ""Believe Me that I am in the Father and the Father is in Me; otherwise believe because of the works themselves. *"Truly, truly, I say to you, he who believes in Me, the works that I do, he will do also; and greater works than these he will do; because I go to the Father.* "Whatever you ask in My name, that will I do, so that the Father may be glorified in   the Son....(Jn 14: 11-13)

124

- El Shaddai (Lord God Almighty)

- Adonai (Lord, Master)

- Yahweh (Lord, Jehovah)

- Jehovah Nissi (The Lord My Banner)

- Jehovah-Raah (The Lord My Shepherd)

- Jehovah Rapha (The Lord That Heals)

- Jehovah Shammah (The Lord Is There)

- Jehovah Tsidkenu (The Lord Our Righteousness)

- Jehovah Mekoddishkem (The Lord Who Sanctifies You)

- Jehovah Jireh (The Lord Will Provide)

- Jehovah Shalom (The Lord Is Peace)

- Jehovah Sabaoth (The Lord of Hosts)

If we are not doing greater works than Jesus, then it suggests that we do not have the faith that He had, remember he walked this earth as a man, so stop saying, oh ya! but he was God, that's why he could do such great miracles. Although it's true that He is a part of the Triune God Head, yet he laid aside His Diety to come to earth as a humble servant in the form of flesh, just like you and me. Like his disciples, we lack faith. Faith comes by hearing and hearing by the word of God. That doesn't mean to read, read, read, *"searching scriptures thinking that in them you have eternal life; and it is these that bear witness of Me; and you are unwilling to come to Me, that you may have life."* (John 5:39,40). Paper or e-books are only words but the Truth within the words is what we want to know, it's the Truth that set us free. Jesus is the Way-Truth-Life. Through Him alone we come to the Father. We study scriptures to rightly divide, to understand them and to look at them as we would look in a mirror to see if the Character of Jesus is fully reflected in our lives, or are their flaws that need God's love applied so that we can grow so that we can reflect His beauty more and more each day.

This course is not about pointing out flaws but about recognizing His Great Love, the Great I AM is LOVE. The real deal! Wow! That's just amazing, His Love is amazing!

Beware! Stay Alert! All of us have not arrived, but are a work in progress until Jesus has perfected His Bride, without spot or wrinkle, then He'll return and we will feast with Him at the Wedding Banquet. For now, here on this earthly plane, in these last days, there are many who are deceived, trapped by their own ego and not conformed into His image. They are prey for the enemy to draw them away from Truth through his various lies and deceptions that are deceitful dainties from the kingdom of this world. *"among them are those who enter into households and captivate weak women weighed down with sins, led on by various impulses, always learning and never able to come to the knowledge of the truth" (2 Tim 3:7)*

We are separated from the I AM manifesting His greatest work through us because of our own weaknesses, our sins, our impulses, our flesh, ego, self. When we can truly die to ourselves completely then we will see greater works than Jesus did and we will have reached the fullness of our inheritance, to be one with the Father. They that hunger and thirst for righteousness will be filled; are you hungry? Let's just do it, let go of ourselves, surrender fully to the Captain of the Hosts of the Army of God. You ain't seen nothing yet; God is doing the greatest work even right now here on this earth. Don't worry about the enemy that's

126

Gods' problem, the wheat and the tares grow up together, but in the midst of it the Church becomes stronger, more united and nothing can stop it! Not even the gates of Hell or any of the enemies pawns.

In my years I've had many experiences listening and obeying God, yet many failures, I am cleaving so close to the I AM, I never want to fail Him or myself again. At one point it was $5 God said to give to someone, it was just obedience; one groceries to a woman I did not know, I found out who she was, where she lived, I brought the groceries to her door, when she opened the door I saw her beautiful home, and thought I'd missed God. So I said sheepishly, "you probably don't need these, but I thought I'd bring a few groceries for you". She broke down crying, grabbed my hand and dragged me to her kitchen. Flinging open the cupboards and fridge, I too nearly cried for I saw nothing, except for a little mustard and relish. She'd been praying for groceries and had told no one, but God heard.

At one point I gave away all of my possessions and moved to Africa, some of you might even be recipients of some of those things. I understand Mother Teresa and her not really wanting possessions but solely desiring God to manifest through her life...and He did!

Don't worry, I'm not saying to give away anything, unless God says, but if He says, do not hesitate, do not rationalize or try to figure it out, just trust Him and obey Him. If you are not sure if it is God, or just your zeal without wisdom consult with your trusted spiritual leader who will bear witness if it the Lord speaking, or speak wisdom into the desire.

Yes we are to study to show ourselves approved, rightly dividing the word of truth

Mind—Will—Emotional Entrainment to the Desires of the Heart of God

-continue to journal your thoughts, dreams, what God is speaking to you as you hunger for righteousness. *"Blessed are those who hunger and thirst after righteousness, for they shall be filled" Mtt 5:6*

Continually live in an attitude of gratitude, thanking the Lord for setting you free and do not allow the devil to discourage you by his condemning whispers to your mind. Sometimes the Lord does a quick work at other times it may be slower. Don't be discouraged even if at times it seems slow or you fail occasionally. Remember, the issue of excess weight came "little by little" and it's healthier to lose it "little by little" rather than yoyo dieting, you want to develop a sustainable plan that you can live with forever. Even a couple of pounds per month equals 24 pounds over the course of a year. In the process you will be developing new habits, character that will eventually become a part of your destiny.

"There is therefore now no condemnation to them which are in Christ Jesus, who walk not after the flesh, but after the Spirit. For the law of the Spirit of life in Christ Jesus hath made me free from the law of sin and death. For what the law could not do, in that it was weak through the flesh, God sending his own Son in the likeness of sinful flesh, and for sin, condemned sin in the flesh: That the righteousness of the law might be fulfilled in us, who walk not after the flesh, but after the Spirit." (Rom 8:1-4)

Finally, utilize the spiritual exercise of fasting periodically as the Lord leads. Even fasting one meal or one day a week will help in disciplining your body to be subject to your spirit man. Perhaps fasting your favourite food or treat, many times the Lord has called me to fast from coffee, which is my favourite drink. What or how often is insignificant, fasting in obedience is what matters to the Lord. *Matthew 6:17-18: "But thou, when thou fastest, anoint thine head, and wash thy face; That thou appear not unto men to fast, but unto thy Father which is in secret: and thy Father, which seeth in secret, shall reward thee openly."*

HOMEWORK: Journal for 7 days your Walking with God leading all the way—Pay continual attention to His Voice of Altruism, a Higher Calling vs Ego or Sin Nature/Fleshly/Base Nature

"My kingdom is not of this world. If My kingdom were of this world, then My servants would be fighting so that I would not be handed over to the Jews; but as it is, My kingdom is not of this realm." (John 18:36)

As we grow in the Lord, he takes us from glory to glory through the things that we suffer. Suffering is not fearful but rather embraced as it was for Jesus because it serves a purpose of spiritual growth within us. Jesus suffered more than any man ever, yet for the joy that was set before him he endured the cross. His kingdom was not of this world. We too are not of this world; our kingdom is a heavenly kingdom. For though we walk in the flesh, we are spirits inhabiting a body for a season; the battle for control over our flesh is not a fleshly battle, it's a spiritual battle.

Each day in your quiet time spend a few moments to record what the Lord is speaking to you regarding your eating, exercise, or health. Pay particular attention to where the Lord has you focus and the feelings that you have while He speaks regarding a specific topic. There is also a space to record any tips that you may have which may not only help you but help others who struggle in their eating habits. This is our last week of class, however, I encourage you to practice journaling as a tool discovering what God is saying to you, it builds faith and provides a record of precious pearls that God reveals to you which will help you help others in their growth. This exercise will give you an opportunity to help others and in so doing you help yourself, for we are truly one body.

DAY 1:

_____

KEY
VERSE:_____

_____

_____

_____

_____

FOCUS:_____

_____

_____

_____

_____

FEELINGS:_____

_____

_____

_____

_____

_____

_____

_____

_____

_____

*TIPS:*_____

_____

_____

_____

_____

_____

DAY2:

_____

KEY
*VERSE:*_____

_____

_____

_____

_____

_____

_FOCUS:_____

_____

_____

_____

_____

_____

_FEELINGS:_____

_____

_____

_____

_____

_____

_TIPS:_____

_____

_____

_____

_____

_____

DAY 3:

_____

KEY
*VERSE:*_____

_____

_____

_____

_____

_____

*FOCUS:*_____

_____

_____

_____

_____

_____

*FEELINGS:*_____

_____

_____

_____

_____

_____

_____

_____

*TIPS:*_____

_____

_____

_____

_____

_____

DAY 4:

_____

KEY
*VERSE:*_____

_____

_____

_____

_____

_____

*FOCUS:*_____

_____

_____

_____

_____

_____

_FEELINGS:_____

_____

_____

_____

_____

_____

_____

_____

_____

_TIPS:_____

_____

_____

_____

_____

DAY 5:

_____

KEY
_VERSE:_____

_____

_____

_____

_____

_____

*FOCUS:*_____

_____

_____

_____

_____

*FEELINGS:*_____

_____

_____

_____

_____

_____

_____

*TIPS:*_____

_____

_____

_____

_____

DAY 6:

_____

KEY
*VERSE:*_____

_____

_____

_____

_____

_____

*FOCUS:*_____

_____

_____

_____

_____

_____

*FEELINGS:*_____

_____

_____

_____

_____

_____

_____

_____

_____

*TIPS:*_____

_____

_____

_____

DAY 7:

_____

KEY
*VERSE:*_____

_____

_____

_____

_____

*FOCUS:*_____

_____

_____

_____

_____

_____

*FEELINGS:*_____

_____

_____

_____

_____

_____

_____

_____

*TIPS:*_____

_____

_____

_____

WEEK #12

OVERCOMERS!

"They overcame by the blood of the Lamb and the word of their testimony"

(Rev 12:11)

The war is fought within our minds. These 12 weeks have been transformational to all who participated wholly with God's Spirit within them, the Great I AM. The victory is ours, it's already been bought by Jesus sacrifice on the cross.

This week is dedicated to sharing our testimonies; we strengthen and encourage each other. We overcome together the works of the enemy in our lives.

"Then I heard a loud voice in heaven, saying, "Now the salvation, and the power, and the kingdom of our God and the authority of His Christ have come, for the accuser of our brethren has been thrown down, he who accuses them before our God day and night. "And they overcame him because of the blood of the Lamb and because of the word of their testimony, and they did not love their life even when faced with death. "For this reason, rejoice, O heavens and you who dwell in them. Woe to the earth and the sea, because the devil has come down to you, having great wrath, knowing that he has only a short time." (Rev 12:10-12)

We've been made more than conquerors, overcomers in this life!

"He that has an ear, let him hear what the Spirit said to the churches..."(Rev 2:7,11,17,26)

"He that overcomes, the same shall be clothed in white raiment and..."(Rev 3:5,12,21)

"These things I have spoken to you, that in me you might have peace..."(Jn 16:33)

"Who shall lay anything to the charge of God's elect? It is God that..." (Rom 8:33-39)

"And the God of peace shall bruise Satan under your feet shortly..."(Rom 16:20)

"But thanks be to God, which gives us the victory through our Lord Jesus Christ"(1 Cor 15:57)

"For though we walk in the flesh, we do not war after the flesh..."(2 Cor 10:3-5)

"Take to you the whole armor of God, that you may be able to withstand.." (Eph 6:13-18)

"I have fought a good fight, I have finished my course, I have kept the faith..."(2 Tim 4:7-8)

"I write to you, fathers, because you have known him that is from..."(1 John 2:13-14)

"You are of God, little children, and have overcome them: because..."(1 John 4:4)

"Who is he that overcomes the world, but he that believes that Jesus..."(1 John 5:5)

We've Been More than Conquerors

1997 Song by

Acappella

We've been made more than conquerors
Overcomers in this life
We've been made victorious
Through the blood of Jesus Christ

When troubles come knockin' at your door
Don't be afraid you know it's not like before
Don't you give in don't let it bring ya down
You don't have to worry anymore

Hold on we're getting stronger ev'ry day
There's no reason for you to go astray
Don't go leaning to your understanding
'cause you don't have to worry anyway

Through the power of Jesus Christ

CONCLUSION

Passover, Jesus the Lamb of God who takes away the sins of the world have mercy on us. As we renew our minds daily, by the washing of the water of the word, which means meditating on the part of the word of God that He illumines to you. It may be only a word, a single verse, a concept, or a story. Just sitting before the Lord, or walking or resting, but attending your heart to what the Spirit of God is saying in that scripture; that is meditating. It's through meditation that our heart is changed and renewed. Too often people read and read, searching scripture thinking that they give eternal life…they don't, they are just words on paper, however, the scripture points to Word, it testifies about Jesus and the finished work of the cross. It is Jesus we seek, He is the Christ door to the Father's Kingdom and His Holy Spirit is His gift to us who believe.

Have this mind that is in Christ Jesus, *"Work hard to show the results of your salvation, obeying God with deep reverence and fear. For God is working in you, giving you the desire and the power to do what pleases him" (Phil 2: 12-13)*

Therefore let him who thinks he stands take heed that he does not fall. No temptation has overtaken you but such as is common to man; and God is faithful, who will not allow you to be tempted beyond what you are able, but with the temptation will provide the way of escape also, so that you will be able to endure it. (1 Cor 10: 12-13)

It is God that hardened Pharoah's heart and God who can purify us.

"I will bring that group through the fire
and make them pure.
I will refine them like silver
and purify them like gold.
They will call on my name,
and I will answer them.
I will say, 'These are my people,'
and they will say, 'The LORD is our God.'"
(Zech 13:9)

"My son, pay attention to what I say;
turn your ear to my words.
Do not let them out of your sight,
keep them within your heart;
for they are life to those who find them
and health to one's whole body.
Above all else, guard your heart,
for everything you do flows from it.
Keep your mouth free of perversity;
keep corrupt talk far from your lips.
Let your eyes look straight ahead;
fix your gaze directly before you.
Give careful thought to the
paths for your feet
and be steadfast in all your ways.
Do not turn to the right or the left;
keep your foot from evil".
(Prov 4: 20-27)

"I have fought the good fight, I have finished the course, I have kept the   faith" (1 Tim 2:4)

Made in the USA
Monee, IL
13 November 2021